2DIE4

2DIE4

ryan DOBSON

with Brian Smith

Multnomah® Publishers *Sisters, Oregon*

TO DIE FOR
published by Multnomah Publishers, Inc.
© 2004 by James Dobson, Inc.

International Standard Book Number: 1-59052-384-9

Interior design and typeset by Katherine Lloyd, The DESK, Bend, OR

Italics in Scripture quotations reflect the author's emphasis.

Scripture quotations are from:
Holy Bible, New Living Translation (NLT)
© 1996. Used by permission of Tyndale House Publishers, Inc.
All rights reserved.
The Holy Bible, *English Standard Version* (ESV)
© 2001 by Crossway Bibles, a division of Good News Publishers.
Used by permission. All rights reserved.
The Holy Bible, New International Version (NIV)
© 1973, 1984 by International Bible Society,
used by permission of Zondervan Publishing House
The Holy Bible, New King James Version (NKJV)
© 1984 by Thomas Nelson, Inc.

Multnomah is a trademark of Multnomah Publishers, Inc.,
and is registered in the U.S. Patent and Trademark Office.
The colophon is a trademark of Multnomah Publishers, Inc.
Printed in the United States of America

For information:
MULTNOMAH PUBLISHERS, INC.
POST OFFICE BOX 1720
SISTERS, OREGON 97759
04 05 06 07 08 09 10—10 9 8 7 6 5 4 3 2 1 0

CONTENTS

Go Phenomenal

On tour, our day starts quiet, but it never stays that way.

We've traveled all night and slept on a big bus, and when we stumble off it, we hardly know what city this is. But here we are. We carry equipment in and set up, and hour by hour the excitement builds.

At last, after the final sound check, we open the doors—and people pour in, so young and energetic and restless and talkative, their faces expectant and alive. I love it. Few of them know who I am, so I mix in the crowd, just getting a feel for them, just listening.

Then it's time. My heart's racing. I jump onstage to pump the crowd and intro the first band, and **I feel the rush.**

The band is great, and soon the crowd's screaming. I see everyone rocking, the mosh pit, the crowd-surfing. Then between bands I'm up in front again, giving short talks about truth and about responsibility and about abstinence. And they're listening. Finally, in front of them one last time before the headliner, I get to speak the gospel, the world's greatest words, the most powerful message in all the universe.

Later I'm at my booth, and a guy or girl comes up to thank me and tell me they've accepted the Lord that night. Based on what *I* said! I'm almost shaking with an incredible, indescribable feeling. I'm freaking out. It's so wild, and I'm thinking what an awesome thrill this is, and **who am I** to be given such an unbelievable privilege?

But it isn't always like that.

SOME DAYS...

There are days on tour when I feel I just can't get up for it. There are times when the crowd's talking while I'm speaking, and I'm sure hardly a soul is hearing me. There are nights when no one comes up afterward to tell me they've come to Christ or that they even liked the message.

And it's not hard at all to start thinking, *It's not supposed to be this way.*

Sometimes I even wonder, *What's the use?*

It's not that I'm under any illusions. Growing up in a Christian home, I figured out a long time ago that the Christian life isn't always a high. It's not like I expect every single moment to be one more rocking, rousing concert climax.

But hey, when you've got certain expectations and suddenly you're staring cold in the face of disappointment...it can be discouraging. Sometimes flat depressing.

I'm betting you know what it's like. And how the flatness and the heaviness can last for a night or hang on for a week or a month. Or, if a person isn't careful, smother your heart for a lifetime.

It can leave you aimless. You used to think you knew what made you happy. Now you wonder what you're looking for.

Life can seem like a job with no job description. They keep telling you, "Here's your life, live it well, you'll be graded when you're done."

You nod. Then you ask, What exactly should I be doing?

"You heard me. Live it well. Succeed. Don't blow it."

But I—

"Just don't blow it!"

Uhh...sure, fine. Okay.

You can end up feeling awfully empty (if you're honest about it). No purpose. I see it everywhere in people's eyes and actions: total boredom.

Not that the world doesn't offer plenty to try and fill the vacuum. There are more diversionary tactics today than ever.

I've got an iPod with four thousand different songs on it (and they make bigger ones than mine). I can listen to music nonstop everywhere I go. For ten straight days I can play songs twenty-four hours a day and never hear the same one twice.

But just in case four thousand different songs begin to bore me, I've still got TV. Hundreds of channels to choose from. Whatever anybody's interested in, they've got a program for it.

I'm into cars, motorcycles, fast stuff. So I can watch *American Hot Rod* or *Monster Garage* or *Junkyard Wars* or *Overhauling* or *Rides*. I can tune in to *The Great Biker Build-Off* with Indian Larry and Billy Lane, *Southern Chopper,* or *Motorcycle Mania* with Jesse James. And more. You name it, they're showing it.

Then when TV gets boring, there's more to move on to. So that's exactly what people do. Party to party. Relationship to relationship. Sexual encounter to sexual encounter. A little alcohol, a lot of alcohol. Drugs to harder drugs. Soft porn to hard-core. Always running to the next thing. Always escaping to the bigger thrill. Always needing a still bigger one.

What a life.

Life? No way. Don't even call it that.

GO TO REALITY

But there is such a thing. **There is such a reality** as an adventure-filled, crazy, awesome, exciting, scary, terrifying, fun-filled *life*. A life that delivers all it promises. Purpose and meaning that never let you down. There really is something—Some*one*—worth dying for, and therefore worth living for, every moment.

I *know* there is. I know such a life is possible, because I'm learning to live it. That's not a prideful statement. I'm not proud of me, because it's a gift to me. And it's offered to you as well. You wanna take it?

That's what this book's about. A life full of excitement. A life to call *phenomenal*. Some lines from a Thousand Foot Krutch song are playing in my head, inviting us all:

CAN'T TAKE IT ANYMORE
SHAKE IT TILL WE MOVE THE FLOOR
WHAT ARE WE WAITING FOR
LET'S GO
TIRED OF BEING ORDINARY
DON'T CARE IF THERE'S PEOPLE STARING
I KNOW YOU SAID YOU'D CARRY ME...ON
I'M NOT INVISIBLE LIKE YOU
NEXT TIME THINGS GET A LITTLE MESSED UP
I'LL SHINE BUT I'LL NEVER BE SEEN THROUGH
I'M FINE JUST TRYING TO WAKE THE REST UP...
DOWN, HERE COMES THE SOUND
EVERYONE POUND YOUR FEET TO THIS PHENOMENON
NOW LET'S MAKE IT LOUD
LET'S SHOW 'EM ALL HOW
YOU MOVE TO THIS PHENOMENON
ROLL! OPEN YOUR SOUL,
MAYBE LOSE CONTROL INSIDE OF THIS PHENOMENON
JUST LET YOURSELF GO
AND LET EVERYONE KNOW
YOU MOVE TO THIS PHENOMENON....
RAISE UP YOUR LIGHTERS
PRAISE TO THE RIGHTEOUS—
NEED YOU TO GUIDE US—
GET PREPARED TO GO

CHAPTER 1

Why Die?

I was actually doing it. Free-falling. My first-ever skydive. Thirteen thousand feet up and plunging toward the ground at 120 miles per hour.

What a rush! I felt an exhilaration bordering on panic. Adrenaline pumped through my body. My senses were heightened.

Now I knew: The things people say to describe how thrilling this is—they're all true. The slipperiness of the atmosphere racing past as you bodysurf on air. The oneness you feel with the sky. The incredible sense of floating on nothing.

The force pushing on your face does crazy things to your looks (I found it out later—another skydiver captured me on video). Meanwhile, you see the panorama of the earth as never before, amazingly cool and soft-edged and peaceful for something that's pulling you closer with enough speed to break every bone in your body on impact.

It was all so insane. I was out of my mind. I was scared.

And I'd never felt so *alive!*

But before getting that far, before that experience could even begin…there was something else I had to do.

I had to jump out of the plane.

Everything people say about that part is true too. Feeling paralyzed at the open door as the wind ripples your jumpsuit. The butterflies throwing a bash in your stomach. Everything inside you screaming, *Are you crazy? Don't do this! You're an idiot!* The icy surge of fear.

After all, it's totally unnatural to step out of an airplane door and fall into nothing.

But without it, without stepping down and out, there'd be no exhilaration of the skydive, no rush of aliveness in the freedom of the wild blue.

That's a good picture of a truth we usually don't want to hear. But it's reality, whether we accept it or not:

To get real life, you first have to die.

OVER THE TOP

That first skydive of mine was just last year. That experience captures well how I feel so often these days.

Yes, I have down days (I'll admit it again). But mostly I've never felt better, because I know I'm doing exactly what I was designed for. I'm in the middle of God's will. I'm a warrior in His battle. And nothing brings greater fulfillment than that.

That's the way it's meant to be for us all.

You probably remember something Jesus told us about it: He invaded this world so we can "have *life* and have it *abundantly.*"[1] Abundant life. Overflowing. Over the top. "Life in all its fullness."[2] Not empty, but full. Not boring or aimless, but going somewhere fast and fun and exciting!

So no matter how much you feel life has burned you or let you down, don't hold back in embracing what Jesus means in that phrase. The life He's offering is an adventure, a quest. It's living in a perpetual, purified panic with your adrenaline pumping. It means going to bed tired but satisfied and optimistic, knowing tomorrow will be filled with significance. Then waking up again with clear direction, with your heart anticipating the day's surprises.

Isn't that what you want?

I know it is.

And the fact is, it's *yours.* It's the essence of the *life* Christ promises throughout the New Testament.

LOSING IT, FINDING IT

But I have to tell you: There's another huge, critical thing Jesus stated about life. Something harder. Something we may forget to think much about.

"Whoever *loses* his life for my sake will find it."

That's something Jesus kept saying again and again.[3] In slightly different ways, but the point was always clear.

To find life…you first have to lose it.

To live…first you die.

Losing your life. Yes, that means dying. How do we know?

Well, in the same breath where Jesus spoke of losing your life, He mentioned "taking up your cross."[4] He didn't mean hanging a piece of jewelry around your neck. Back then, the cross wasn't a trinket; it was a form of execution. It would be like telling somebody today, **Have a seat in this electric chair.** Or, "Hey, let's go stand in front of that firing squad."

One other time when Jesus talked about losing your life, He told a tiny little story with a tiny little hero. Actually He tells the story in two versions.

In one version, the tiny little hero falls into a terrible place that was deep and dark. He's all shut in and shut down. Covered over, in fact, with dirt. Dead and buried. But there's an incredibly happy ending (more about that later).

In the other version, the tiny little hero manages to avoid falling into that terribly dark and deep place. But this version of the story is a tragedy. Why? Because that tiny little guy was alone, and *stayed* alone…forever. All because he wouldn't fall into that terrible, deadly, dark place.

The hero is actually a seed. Jesus told the story this way (a lot quicker than I did): "Truly, truly, I say to you, unless a grain of wheat falls into the earth and dies, it remains alone; but if it dies, it bears much fruit."[5] This "bearing much fruit" is just another way of saying "abundant life."

That's the incredible happy ending for the little hero who let himself die.

Jesus told this story only a day or so before He Himself would hang on a cross and be killed. He was telling that story about Himself. But He was also telling it about you and me. Because He quickly went on to say, "If anyone serves me, he must follow me; and where I am, there will my servant be also."[6]

Where He is, we're to be. Jesus is saying, Because *I* go to the cross, I want *you* to go to the cross. **If I die, you die.** If you're really My follower, My servant, then you have no other option.

ACTUAL DYING?

But you're thinking, This doesn't literally mean dying, does it? As in, no more breathing, no more heartbeats. As in actually getting killed. Does it?

It might. Someday, it just might. For you, and for me.

And if it does, and we're willing, and there's no question in our soul that Jesus is worth dying for…then one thing we can know for sure: **He'll get us ready for it.** When the moment comes, He'll make sure we're brave and calm. And it will mean glory and honor unimaginable. (We'll also talk about that in this book.)

Meanwhile, until that day comes (*if* it comes)…there's a lot of other dying for you and me to do. The kind that doesn't stop your breathing or your heart…but it's still dying. Funny how the Bible insists on calling it that. It doesn't say "adjust." It doesn't say "tweak your behavior." It doesn't say "modify your identity." It doesn't say "evolve your personhood." It says *die*. And keep dying. (We'll talk a lot about this too.)

I'll shoot straight: This second kind of dying is as hard as the other kind. It's scary. It can be painful and usually is. It doesn't feel good; it never gets pleasurable in and of itself. That's why it's right to call it *death*.

But Jesus gets us ready for this kind too.

And this second kind of dying brings glory and honor as well. It leads to its own out-of-your-mind thrill. Its own free-falling rush. It brings such a scary, insane, exhilarating adventure that you can't help saying, **"I've never felt so alive!"**

And then you'll know, beyond the shadow of a doubt, that it's more than worth it…to keep stepping out that door into nothing.

CHAPTER 2

Crave the Fear

Hard-core sports guys like to say that unless your sport could get you killed, it isn't really a sport. It's just a game.

I'd say that's pretty true about life too. If it isn't high-end dangerous, if it isn't risky, if it isn't scary…it's not really living. It's only a game.

Down deep, we all know this is true (if we're honest). You and I were born for excitement and adventure.

Ultimately we can be satisfied with nothing less than the adrenaline-filled life. Anything less leaves us bored. And when we're bored, we're boring.

Even to God.

Jesus once said He'd rather we be cold or hot than luke-warm. *Lukewarm* means just air-temperature. You're un-hot, you're un-cold. You're simply the same temperature as your environment. Your atmosphere controls you. Your personal spiritual thermostat is disengaged or out of order, so you generate no heat of your own. You're just the slave of your surroundings. You let your background blend you in. You just go with the flow.

When you're like that, Jesus said He feels like vomiting you right out of His mouth.[7]

Fact is, you sometimes feel the same way about yourself. You hate being bored, don't you? An aimless, boring, empty existence seems hardly worth it.

BEYOND THE LIMITS

So what takes away the boringness and the aimlessness?

Risk.

Danger.

The real potential to actually die.

When we're honest about how we're all wired, we know how much we need to break beyond protective limits. To plunge over the edge. To push for the impossible. *To crave the fear.*

And to escape from what's safe, predictable, easy.

Deep inside, we're looking for something that's truly worth a total sacrifice.

But not just any risk is right. Not just any danger will do. Not just any potential for death is worth it.

Satan deludes plenty of people into living and dying for wrong causes. Anything from a stupid dare at a party to a worldwide terrorism plot. Satan doesn't care whether he hooks you one way or another. He'll claim a person's life any way he can.

Satan's specialty has always been to suck people into losing their lives for misguided and meaningless causes. Just like Jesus said: The devil has always been a lying murderer.[8]

But Jesus rescued you and me from the devil's death-grip. And when we first believed in Christ and He actually took up residence inside us through His Spirit, He planted the right stuff within us. He planted deep inside us the desire to spend our entire existence *for the right cause only.* The very fact that you're reading this book is evidence of that. (And maybe it would be good if you thanked Him for it.)

THE RIGHT CAUSE

Notice I said **THE right cause.**

Because ultimately, there's only one.

Christ gives you the true longing to give your life only for *Him.* He Himself is the only worthy cause. That's why when Jesus told us to lose our lives, He said to do it "for My sake."[9]

Any other cause that's truly worth giving your life for will be worth it only because Jesus Himself personally called you to that assignment.

Let's think hard about this.

"Christ lives in me"[10]—the Bible teaches us to know that fact by faith. *He's* inside you. Not as some junior-grade

Jesus. Not as a miniature version. Not as an immature Jesus who'll need lots of time to grow up. No, **inside you is Christ as He fully exists.**

That's the same Jesus Christ who rose from the dead. The same Jesus who walked on water and calmed storms and healed the sick and taught with authority. The same Jesus who said that anyone who believes in Him would do this stuff too, and even greater stuff.[11]

Impossible? Absolutely. But God specializes in the impossible.

HIS MIND, YOUR MIND

Now grab hold of this:

If *Christ* is there inside you, then so are His plans and dreams and goals and ambitions for your life. The Bible teaches us to know and to say, "We have the mind of Christ."[12] His mind, of course, holds His vision and His strategies for all you can be and do in life. It's a vision that goes far beyond anything you could express or imagine.[13] It's a vision and a strategy for a profound, powerful life. He holds it all. And by staying connected with Him, we learn to see it all. We think what He thinks.

That's why Jesus is not just our best example of a power-living person. He's the actual *source* for our own power-living. In fact, He's now carrying out *His* power-living through *us*.

People today can no longer see Jesus in the body He

had when He walked on earth. But He continues to live out His life in *our* bodies. So that now—more than ever—the world can see Jesus at work.

You can be a part of it. You're *meant* to be a part of it. The whole package is already there inside you. It's God's gift to you (through the living Holy Spirit), just waiting to be opened and released.

And once it is, and you know exactly what He's called you to do in life, you can be satisfied with nothing less.

A JUNKIE'S LIFE

A junkie's only thought is about where the next fix is coming from.

I know, because **I'm a junkie. I admit it.** I'm an adrenaline junkie. And I'm a junkie for Christ. My heart is so fixated on the calling of Christ that I'm dying to feel it more and more. Stronger and stronger. I'd do anything to continue that feeling, and that means doing whatever God calls me to do. Fulfilling my purpose.

And I know my purpose.

Here's a statement that I keep with me in written form at all times: "I was born to testify to the truth." It's from words that Jesus spoke just before He was sentenced to die.[14] This statement is my creed, my calling.

I've got a panic, an urgency, a desperation to go out and spread the gospel. To testify to the truth. That's the message God has given me. That's what He's called me to. If I don't do it, I know the consequences could be severe (I haven't forgotten why Jonah got swallowed by a fish).

So I do a lot of traveling and speaking. Not long ago I had a stretch where I spoke 50 times in 55 days. At one point I spoke at three different events in less than twenty-four hours. My parents tell me I'm crazy to keep up that pace. They say I can't do this forever.

They're right. I can't do it forever. But **I can do it now.** And I'm called to do it now.

So I crave every opportunity to help hurting and lost people. I have a hard time saying no to speaking engagements. This cause is everything to me. And if Christ's call to this ministry means I never get married again or have a family, I'm willing to give that up.

As God shows you what He's called you to, I want you to be inflamed with the same urgency and panic and desperation about it that I have. And I know that if you'll trust Him, He'll give you exactly that.

THIS COULD GET YOU KILLED

Let me say something again, because it's so radically huge. This is at the very heart of who you really are as a believer in Christ: *When you became a Christian, God placed inside you the desire to live all-out for the Lord.* That longing is there because of Jesus Himself living inside you, through His Holy Spirit.

Yep, you can dull that desire. You can choose to hide it,

bury it, deny it. But why do something so stupid? Why not nurture that desire instead? Why not unleash it? Why not let it explode? **Why not let it take you** to excitement beyond your wildest dreams?

Why not let the Spirit of Jesus ignite within you the power and boldness and courage to crave the fear. To crave the risk. To crave the danger. To experience the adrenaline rush.

Will the risk be real?

Without a doubt.

Could it get you killed?

Of course.

So that's what we'll talk more about next.

CHAPTER 3

The Long, Long Line

We've touched on it. Now let's hit it straight on.

It's the really major issue. The huge one. So big, it's overwhelming. No way we can handle this topic on our own, or fully grasp all it means. But I know God wants us to think it through carefully.

It's the matter of actually *losing our physical life* for the Lord. The total sacrifice. Going all the way. And our willingness to do it.

If we can start to sort this out, then who knows? Maybe everything else required in our Christian lives will fall into place a little easier for us.

So first, let's tackle a few questions that might be on your mind.

AREN'T THOSE DAYS OVER?

The time in history when lots of people were killed just for being a Christian—isn't that all in the past? Or at least *mostly* in the past? Sure, it probably still happens from time to time, here and there. But in general, hasn't the world gotten a lot more easygoing than that?

The answer's no. **Absolutely not.**

Persecution against Christians is far from over. In fact, it's getting worse.

If you doubt me on that, I strongly encourage you to read *Jesus Freaks* and *Jesus Freaks, Volume II*, both by dc Talk and Voice of the Martyrs. And visit www.persecution.org, the website for International Christian Concern. You'll discover that the number of Christians dying for Jesus' sake is now more than at any time in history—over 160,000 each year![15]

If that's a surprise to you, I think I know why. Like most people reading this book, you're probably an American, or at least a westerner. Not many (if any) of the people you know are ever threatened with death just for being a believer in Jesus. But in lots of places on this planet—especially in Africa and Asia, where most of the world's people live—**that threat is real.** As real as the air you're breathing this moment.

According to one estimate, 200 million Christians are actively persecuted for their faith, while another 400 million are under serious restrictions just for being Christians.[16] That's a total of 600 million persecuted Christians—one-tenth of the entire world's population!

If you're hardly aware of this, maybe it's because you're stuck in your culture's deliberate isolation from many aspects of reality. You see, our western news media will usually try to ignore or at least downplay these things. (Their agendas tend to be anti-Christian—subtly but strongly.)

Fortunately we have other sources (like Voice of the Martyrs) to keep us better informed.

CAN'T GOD DO A BETTER JOB OF PROTECTING US?

God can of course fully protect His people from death and persecution. So why doesn't He do a better job of it? Why are so many Christians getting killed? Has His strategy for His church gone haywire? Are things out of control?

No, everything's right on schedule.

Think about it. God could have kept Jesus from getting crucified. When He was arrested, Jesus announced that His Father could instantly send twelve legions of angels to His side. That's about 72,000 blazing angel-warriors with swords of fire. Plenty to roast every enemy in sight.

To bring on this angel army, all Jesus had to do was ask His Father for them.

So why didn't He?

Right on the spot, Jesus explained it: "If I did, how would the Scriptures be fulfilled?"[17] In that moment for Jesus there was **something more important than staying alive.**

Jesus was fulfilling God's *plan.* A perfect plan laid out in Scripture. Jesus knew that this plan called for the Son of God to be killed. And in loving obedience to His Father, Jesus yielded to it.

What about God's plan for *us*—especially as it relates to

dying for our faith? Do the Scriptures offer a clue?

More than a clue. All over the Bible you'll find plenty of reminders that Christians are called to suffer for Christ—to share in *His* sufferings.

And there's more. In Revelation 6, we glimpse an amazing scene in heaven. Those who have already been killed for Christ are crying out to God. They're asking Him how much longer it will be till all this is over and God judges the world.

The answer they get should make you **pause and think.** God told them they needed "to rest a little longer until *the full number* of their brothers and sisters—their fellow servants of Jesus—had been martyred."[18] *Martyred.* I don't have to tell you that He's talking about being killed for Christ.

God's plan for this world calls for a certain number of Christians to be put to death for the sake of Jesus. That number is *not* small. It's huge. Enormous. God knows exactly who's on that list, and how many names there are. Until that number's reached—until all the names are checked off—the killing will continue.

And we haven't reached it yet. **We're still not there.** Even though tens of millions of Christians down through the centuries have already been put to death. Even though, in the twenty-first century, 160,000 more names get checked off on the list every year.

That's God's purpose. That's His amazing, mysterious plan. And it's all part of the good and perfect story He's written for us, a story that will make Him more famous than ever when we finally see how it all plays out.

When Christians die, God hasn't lost control. When they die in greater numbers than ever before, it's not because His design for world history has been sidetracked. No way.

Rather, it's because His plan is being fulfilled now more than ever.

And what could be more exciting?

WHO'S ON THAT LIST?

Come join me in a wild dream. Imagine we're stepping up to some giant parchment scroll in heaven. It must weigh tons.

It's guarded by blazing angel-warriors, so you and I get those big guys to help us open the scroll. Together we roll out the first few feet of parchment. There's a title at the beginning:

Followers of Jesus Christ
Who Will Be Killed for His Sake

Under that heading, we spot the first listing:

1. Stephen

You've heard of that guy. So have I. The first martyr. First in a long line. We've read his story in the Bible, in the book of Acts. And right there's his name at the top of the list. Yet this roster was written *before* Stephen died as Martyr Number One.

Dude, this is one old, old, scroll!

We roll it out a little farther. (Thank you, angel-warriors!) We're looking closely. You're the first to spot Paul's name. There it is, in the ancient, clear handwriting. Then I show you Peter's name. It isn't long until we've come across the names of just about every Christian we've read about in the New Testament.

Those were dangerous days to be a Christian, all right.

But it looks like **the danger didn't die.** We keep rolling out the scroll. On and on and on. It stretches literally for miles. Millions upon millions of names. Year after year. Century upon century.

We finally get to the twentieth-first century. The list keeps going. Thousands and thousands of men and women and girls and boys who would be chosen by God to be martyred for Christ in 2001, in 2002, in 2003, in 2004...

In this part, many of the names sound African. A ton of Chinese names too, and other Asian names. We've heard how the church of Jesus Christ is thriving in places like China and Africa. We've heard how passionate and strong the faith of many believers is in those places. We've heard how it often puts the faith of western Christians to shame by comparison.

But what if God allowed His church in the west to become as passionately alive as the church is in other parts of the world?

You and I talk about that. It would probably mean lots more persecution for western Christians. And that would mean we'll find lots more western names on this scroll, if we keep unrolling it to look into the future.

We look each other in the eye. You're thinking what I'm thinking: *Let's go for it.*

We turn back to the scroll. We unroll it some more.

You're wondering, **Will my name be here?**

My thoughts exactly—about *my* name, that is.

Inch by inch, we keep unrolling the ancient parchment. But suddenly…we wake up.

Dream's over. Leaving our last question unanswered.

Guess we're gonna have to wait and find out the hard way.

ISN'T THIS ONLY FOR HEROES?

But hey, maybe our names aren't on that scroll after all. Isn't that list reserved for real hero types?

Yes and no.

Logic says no. With so many millions of names on that roster, they can't *all* be Superman.

Did you know that the Greek word *martyr* simply means "witness"? It doesn't take much to qualify to die for Jesus. All you have to do is be a witness for Him by your words and by your life.

In parts of the world, that's all it takes right now to get a whiplash on your back or a gun to your head or a knife against your chest.

So **does that make you a hero?** Are you some kind of champion if all you do is speak honestly about what Jesus does for you? If you admit that you're a sinner headed for hell, but that Jesus died for you to pay your penalty? That He rose from the dead and you know He's alive today?

Do you deserve a medal if you simply make known the fact that Jesus is alive in your life, letting you know what to say and what to do? That He's giving you strength and peace and security like you've never known before? That He lets you accomplish what you otherwise never could in your own weakness and limitations?

Is it some great heroic deed to tell somebody Jesus is waiting for you in heaven, and you're going to live with Him there forever?

Is that really so extraordinary?

If you and I honestly admit the basic truth about our lives, and somebody else is stupid enough to kill us for it...does that make us a hero?

In the Lord's eyes...**yes!**

In the Lord's eyes, every faithful witness is a champion to be honored. And He'll *personally* honor them when they reach heaven: "The Lamb in the midst of the throne will be their shepherd, and he will guide them to springs of living water, and God will wipe away every tear from their eyes."[19]

Our persecution here may bring plenty of tears. But it

will be more than worth it to have God Himself wipe them away in heaven.

SO SHOULD I TRY TO
GET MYSELF KILLED?

One last question: Is it right to go out and *try* to get ourselves killed for Christ?

No.

God never tells us to actively seek martyrdom. That would be a lot like suicide, and suicide isn't in God's playbook for us. True sacrifice, yes. Selfish suicide, no. (By the way, suicide is nothing more than one of the highest forms of selfishness possible. It always is. Even the suicide-bomber thing that hyped-up terrorists do. And Satan revels in it. So don't ever get caught thinking that suicide is so brave and noble.)

The fact is, true believers in Christ love life more than anyone else possibly can. That's because they see and enjoy *real* life. They recognize God's hand in everything around them. They know God created all life and everything in this world, and that He created it all *good*. **They love it here,** while at the same time they're eager to see Jesus in heaven—on *His* timing, not theirs.

On the other hand, if the moment to die for Jesus comes, they won't draw back.

On that big scroll we looked at, one of the most famous names from the second century was that of

Ignatius. This man served as a bishop to Christians in Syria, on the eastern edge of the Roman Empire. When the Roman emperor gave a fresh decree that everyone should worship Roman gods, Ignatius was one of many who publicly refused. The emperor was visiting Syria at the time, and Ignatius was arrested and dragged before him.

The emperor found him guilty. Ignatius was condemned to be taken to Rome and eaten by wild beasts in the Coliseum.

Hearing this sentence, Ignatius did not stand there whimpering for mercy. He didn't weep at his misfortune. Instead **he hugged his chains** and shouted thanksgiving to God. (Okay, so maybe this guy really *was* a hero, in every sense of the word.)

Ignatius was worried about something, however. He was afraid that when he finally reached Rome (it was a long journey), the many Christians there would publicly rise to his defense and perhaps persuade the authorities to give him a lighter sentence. So Ignatius wrote to the Roman Christians and begged them *not* to speak up for him.

"I die willingly for God, provided you do not interfere," he wrote. He said that even if he lost his nerve when he got to Rome and started begging for their help, he wanted them not to listen to him.

But he fully expected to stay strong. He said that if for some reason the wild beasts held back from attacking him, he would coax them on. "I will even coax them to make short work of me," he said—he wanted them to devour him so completely that little or nothing was left of him to bury.

His longing was granted. In about the year 110 A.D., Ignatius was brought into the Coliseum on a December day, and the wild beasts were let loose. When they finished with him, only a few bones were left.

ASKING TOO MUCH?

But maybe by now, you're thinking this martyrdom thing is an awful lot to ask. It's going overboard. **Too extreme.**

You're thinking, It's not that Jesus doesn't deserve it from us. It's not that it's too much for Him to ask. After all, He already died for us. Why shouldn't we do it for Him?

But maybe here's your hesitation:

I just don't know if I've got the nerve or the backbone or whatever it takes to really lose my life for His sake—if and when it really comes to that.

So how do we get what it takes? What can give us that nerve? Where do we find the backbone?

Let's talk about it next.

CHAPTER 4
Risk Explosion

You're seated alone at a little round table in a conference room. You're waiting for a job interview, and you're stoked about it. That's why you came early.

You've heard this position is incredible. Lots of exciting, fulfilling projects. Travel to thrilling places. A great team of coworkers. Plus benefits that are out of this world.

You desperately want it all.

But first you've got to make it through an interview with your potential boss.

You're nervous as all get-out. You wipe your hand across your forehead and temples. Damp with sweat. You shoot up a quick prayer that it won't drip on the table in the middle of the interview. You pull your arms close to your side to hide your soaked armpits.

Right on time, a man walks in wearing a genuine smile. He greets your warmly. This guy's got to be terribly busy, but he actually seems glad to take time with you.

Probably an incredible boss, you're thinking. What a dream job this would be!

He casually sits down across the table from you and encourages you to tell him about yourself.

You lean forward and start explaining a few of your many qualifications.

READY ANY MOMENT

As you describe yourself to this man, his response is—well, a bit surprising. It's not that he seems all that impressed with the personal strengths you mention. It's more like he's just interested in absolutely everything about you. His eyes light up as you speak. He seems fully accepting and appreciative of who you really are. You feel you could tell him anything—even your faults—and he'd never flinch.

You lean back in your chair. You're not sweating anymore. You spread out your elbows on the chair's armrests. He's put you totally at ease.

Man, **you'd die to work for this guy.**

You decide that maybe you should politely ask your potential boss a relevant question, and stop talking about yourself. (To show how polite you are. And how relevant.)

"If I may," you say, with a slight tilt of your head, "can I ask what's most important for me to understand about this job, in your opinion?"

He nods. His smile widens. (You're thinking, *Score! Way to ask a cool question.*)

He leans closer. "I'd like you to know something about me." His voice is tender and deep. "Long ago, I once had to endure a horrible ordeal. I won't go into details. But I received some extremely severe injuries. I'll always have the scars."

Your heart goes out to him. "Really?" you ask. You're immediately aware of how strong this man appears. It's hard to even imagine him hurt or physically impaired in any way.

"Yes, it's true," he answers. "And I'd like to ask you to be willing—if you take this position—to let the same thing happen to you."

Long, silent pause. Did you hear him correctly? You open your mouth to ask, but the words won't come. You're staring into his eyes. They're deep as the ocean.

He speaks more softly: "I would like you to be ready at any moment to undergo the same treatment I did. As a matter of fact, in this position you might be called on to endure that treatment again and again, for as long as you're here."

So. You did hear him correctly.

You close your mouth. You gulp hard.

He's staring at you with those eyes.

You're sweating again. You wipe your forehead. You pull your arms in tighter to your side.

And you're thinking…maybe this isn't the dream job you thought it was.

NOT NORMAL

What could possibly make you (or anybody) accept such a position?

Maybe only this:

It would take getting to know that guy a whole lot better. And in the process, you'd have to discover that he was totally the most caring, loving, and trustworthy friend and leader you could ever serve.

For a person that good, you could at least *start* to be willing to suffer injury.

But to be willing to actually *die* for him…now that would probably take more. You'd have to know him even better. Most likely you'd have to become convinced—totally, absolutely—that *he* was willing to die for you as well.

It's only natural to think that way. The Bible confirms it: "No one is likely to die for a good person," the apostle Paul said, "though someone might be willing to die for a person who is especially good."[20]

And here's something interesting. That passage goes on to say this:

"But God showed his great love for us by sending Christ to die for us while we were still sinners."[21]

Whoa, **Jesus broke the mold.** He didn't die for people who were exceptionally good. Not even for people who were fairly good. He died for bad people. Sinners. Like you and me.

It's not normal. But He did it.

So that's something we can know for certain about Him. He'd die for us. He already proved it.

GRACIOUS AND BLUNT

In that job interview story, Jesus of course is the strong dude with the smile and the scars. He's the one checking us out for the job of being His follower. He's the one who'll be our leader, telling us what to do and how to do it.

The position He offers is awesome. Work that's exciting and fulfilling. Thrilling travel sometimes. An unbeatable team of coworkers. Plus out-of-this-world benefits.

And as our boss, He also demands—graciously and lovingly, but firmly—that we be willing to die for Him.

He warned His disciples about it. He was blunt: "You will be handed over to be persecuted and put to death, and you will be hated by all nations because of me."[22] **This wasn't scare tactics from Jesus.** It all really happened to these guys (in the years to come).

The topic kept coming up as Jesus trained His men:

"You will be betrayed even by parents, brothers, relatives and friends, and they will put some of you to death."[23]

"Remember the words I spoke to you: 'No servant is greater than his master.' If they persecuted me, they will persecute you also."[24]

"In fact, a time is coming when anyone who kills you will think he is offering a service to God."[25]

He's just as blunt while training you and me. He tells us, "Be faithful, *even to the point of death,* and I will give you the crown of life."[26]

But it's all backed up with His own sacrifice for us. He gave *His* life for us. He took that risk.

RISK EXPLOSION

And now that risk is exploding. The danger didn't shrivel up and blow away when Jesus died. Yes, the authorities caught their man; they put their criminal in the grave, all right. Trouble is, He didn't stay there.

So the danger didn't die. It intensified. All because of *Him.*

It's "for My name's sake," Jesus said, that we face persecution and death.[27] Don't miss those words. Do you see what's happening? *He takes all the blame* for this deadly danger that threatens us.

I know something about that danger. I've seen it up close. Because of my dad's prominence (and threats against him), I got my first bulletproof vest when I was fifteen. I'm about to go on a speaking tour, and in addition to my vest (have you noticed how bulky it makes me look?), I'll be followed everywhere by a security detail.

My dad and the rest of my family have had to take these kinds of precautions for many years, as we stay committed to God's truth. Dad knows that his message about what needs to change in our culture and our country is intensely hated by many. But he's so committed to the call of God upon him that he continues, even in the face of such threats. He stays on the path Jesus put him on.

Jesus knew the risk would explode for everyone who believes in Him. That's why He spells it out for us. He knows that the very fact of believing in Him is gonna stir up lots of trouble for us.

So don't get mad at me if you're not liking this business about having to lose your life. It wasn't my idea. It's just part of what we share when we identify with Jesus. Because the world happens to hate Him and what He stands for. We can all be grateful that He's clear and up front in telling us about it. He tells us that this is reality, and He tells us why.

So are we buying it?

WHEN THIS GETS EASY

Let's face it.

Right now, a lot of this is only words on paper. (For many of us, anyway, if we're honest.) This stuff about Jesus dying for us, and about that becoming some great huge motivation for us to be willing to lose our lives. It just doesn't work out that way so nice and easy.

Does it?

Even if we *want* it to work that way…it isn't automatic. Is it?

If it's only a *concept*—if it's only something we've heard about and read about and even sung about and maybe even thanked God for—if that's *all* it is, then that's not nearly enough to make you or me or anyone else willing to die for Jesus Christ.

I think it takes more.

A whole lot more.

We've got to actually come to *know* Him. And fall in love with Him.

Then it gets…then it actually becomes…

Easy.

Jesus is calling you to come and die for Him. It's true. No doubt about it. But are you hearing Him say more than that?

You will, if you get quiet enough and close enough. And when you do, the dying part will seem like a privilege, not a burden. Like a joy instead of a drag.

More and more in love with Him…means more and more willing to die for Him.

Jesus is not just looking for compliant martyr candidates. He's looking for hearts that are passionately in love with Him. He's looking for the kind of obedience-to-the-death that's driven by our consuming worship and devotion to Him. A worship and devotion that are nurtured by seeing Him and hearing Him, and being amazed and awestruck by what we see and hear.

So do whatever it takes to let Him draw near to you. Do whatever it takes to really get to know Him.

Do anything to hear His loving voice.

Get still before Him. Get quiet. Get rid of the distractions. (You know what they are.)

Go away somewhere and don't come back until you've read through the entire New Testament or even the whole Bible—if that's what it takes.

Or read just one page, or one paragraph, or one line in the "red letters" of the Gospels. Read it over and over and over. Until you know you're hearing His voice.

Pray for Him to speak to you. Plead for it. Thank Him for it, even before it comes, to prove your faith.

And remember how He wants to hear your voice, too.

So confess your sins. He'll show them to you. He'll show you blindness and hardness and rebellion in your life. If you let Him, He'll show you exactly where you've been grieving Him. It's not hidden from Him. He just wants to hear you admit it. He wants to help you come clean.

And then listen. Keep your Bible open, and really *listen*. He has so much to tell you—His friend and child and loyal servant—about His plans for you. Plans that may include death. Plans that for sure include the willingness to die.

And as you learn more about it, you won't be sweaty or nervous. You'll only be amazed and grateful that He counts you worthy for such a job.

CHAPTER 5

Hostile Fire

Recreational skydiving centers like to advertise their services with lines like these:

"Get ready for the most exciting time of your life!"

"Skydiving lets you live life to the fullest!"

They sound like me. I've already told you what an awesome experience I had my first time free-falling up there.

Now picture this situation: Just like I was, you're standing at the plane door ready to jump. Wind ripples through your jumpsuit. Your stomach does somersaults. The fear surges. But you take the plunge. You step out and fall into nothing.

You're thousands of feet up, free-falling. Gravity's sucking you downward, 120 miles per hour. You feel exhilaration. The rush of panic. Adrenaline pumping.

At the right altitude, you pull the ripcord and your chute opens. You sense this amazing relief as the canopy blossoms full above you. Beautiful sight. You're just floating now on the nothingness of air.

Cool. (Birds get to do this all the time, you're thinking; that's why they sing.)

Oh—but I forgot one detail: This is wartime. Your drop zone happens to be behind enemy lines. You were planning to come down in an isolated area. But you've been spotted. You can't see the enemy, but they easily see you.

And they're firing.

Suddenly your adventure has gotten complicated.

NOT A GAME

You and I both know we face a real spiritual enemy. That means conflict. Battle and war. And where there's war, there's death. (That is, as long as the soldiers are willing to fight to the death. Otherwise, there's only surrender. Capitulation.)

In sports, your biggest battle is always against yourself and your own physical and mental barriers and limitations. You try to push beyond them. You also struggle against other contestants or other teams. You battle their strengths and skills and strategies. It's all a lot of fun.

But **life is not a sport.** Life is real warfare. Actual combat. With actual casualties. It's a murderous war because our enemy is deadly.

Our enemy's only goal is to strip your very life from you. He comes after us only "to steal and kill and destroy."[28] He wants to rob us of all the life which the Lord gives us. That's his favorite way to get back at God, his Maker and Judge.

Satan wants us dead.

And he hunts us down with a vengeance.

Literally.

And if you think this enemy isn't hunting *you*...if you think you haven't really caught his attention...then maybe he's already won a greater influence and victory over you than you realize. That's one of his most common and successful strategies—to make you think he isn't *personally* threatening *you*.

Let me warn you with the Bible's warning: "Be self-controlled and alert. Your enemy the devil prowls around like a roaring lion looking for someone to devour."[29] He prowls. And he devours. All with more deceptive tactics than you can imagine. He's so skilled at diversion and trickery that millions of Christians spend most of their lifetime unaware that they're even in a war zone. In effect, the enemy has already devoured them.

UGLIER THAN YOU THOUGHT

I'll bet you didn't miss the Balrog in *The Lord of the Rings*. That massive, fiery monster who fought with Gandalf in the Mines of Moria. When he blasted on the scene, there was instant action. The good guys could flee him or fight him, **but they couldn't just stand there** and ignore him.

It was different with Grima Wormtongue. Remember him? That snaky, sniveling adviser who managed to paralyze

Rohan's King Theoden. He quietly lurked around. And people tolerated him. They didn't like him particularly, but they didn't find him as dangerous as an orc or a troll.

Yet the evil this slimy guy accomplished was more devastating than anything the Balrog did. Under Wormtongue's spell, King Theoden became a zero—mentally, spiritually, physically. As a result, his kingdom of Rohan for a long time did nothing against the forces of Mordor that were ready to overrun the kingdom.

J. R. R. Tolkien didn't write *The Lord of the Rings* for entertainment value alone. He wanted to wake up the world to the deadly war raging around us and within us every day of our lives.

The enemy we face is far more fearsome and ugly and powerful than anything we saw on the screen in *Lord of the Rings*. He's sneakier than Grima Wormtongue and more violent and furious than the Balrog. He and his demons are locked in constant, intense, life-and-death warfare with the armies of God.

And Christians are his number one targets.

SUBTLE STRATEGIES

I don't know how much credit to give demonic forces for all the hardships that pester my ministry efforts. But I do know that even when demons don't cause the problem, they still try to use it to plant seeds of discontent and bitterness in my heart.

If they can catch me hungry or tired or sick or hurt or depressed, they whisper words of doubt into my mind and try to convince me the thoughts are my own:

You're not good enough to serve God.

God doesn't want you.

What makes you think you're anything special?

I've also seen the enemy harass and tempt people close to me—friends who support and encourage me while I face the spiritual fight we're all called to.

This isn't a chess game. **The demons don't abide by nice, neat rules.** This is guerilla warfare—nasty, dirty, all-out, no-holds-barred street fighting. And we need to be as ready as possible. The enemy will hurt our families, threaten our lives, tempt us with filth, or get us hung up on some stupid worry—whatever he thinks will work.

NETWORK OF DARKNESS

And then the bad news gets worse.

The evil we face is present not only in the forms of Satan and his demons. The evil has also taken over and saturated this world we live in. "The whole world lies in the power of the evil one."[30]

The book of Revelation shows us eerie visions of beasts and dragons and the prostitute of Babylon. It's an incredible picture of how Satan and his demons and this world system are so closely intertwined in a network of darkness.

This evil world system is a lot like *The Matrix*—**a powerful, impersonal system** run by Satan, designed to control our minds and our lives.

As just like in *The Matrix,* the world contains billions of victims who are all under enemy control. Christians are here to love and rescue them, but the enemy can use them against us. So even as we try to help the lost, we may find ourselves defending ourselves against them.

But don't be afraid of people. They themselves are victims of the world, the flesh, and Satan.

ENEMY WITHIN

And the news gets even worse.

The evil also saturates *us*—in our sinful nature. It's what the New Testament calls *the flesh*. It's the enemy within— the part of each of us that keeps wanting to sin. Paul explains that the flesh and the Holy Spirit are constantly at each other's throats, as the flesh commits sins of the body, mind, and spirit.[31]

This "flesh" part of us is also intricately interconnected with the world's system of evil: "For everything in the world—the cravings of sinful man, the lust of his eyes and the boasting of what he has and does—comes not from the Father but from the world."[32]

Even well-meaning Christians can let themselves be **brainwashed and used** by the world system to fight against each other. I know, because I've often been attacked by fellow believers. Even worse, I've often played right into the enemy's hand and let him use me to harm my brothers and sisters.

ARE YOU WANTED FOR MURDER?

This world wants us to soothe and pamper ourselves. This world demands that we stay committed to our selfishness. And if we don't go along, this world rages against us. The world hates us if we do what God tells us to do about the flesh, which is to slay it. (We'll talk more about that later.)

Imagine somewhere the world's largest courtroom. The world itself is the judge and jury and prosecutor. And the world is dragging every single Christian into that courtroom, one by one. As each believer goes in and steps forward for his or her trial, the following charge is read aloud: "Instead of pampering your selfish ego, instead of nurturing your lustful and prideful flesh—you tried to kill it! **You stand accused** of committing the unnatural act of attempted murder!"

If your turn came to walk in there and stand trial on that charge...is there enough evidence to convict you? Would they quickly discover that you're a trained killer...of your ego, of your selfish "rights," of your lusts, of your insistent pride? Of your love of comfort and pleasure? Of your go-with-the-flow complacency?

Or would they find that you're really not that much different from non-Christians?

THE BATTLE RAGES

I'll say it again: The evil enemy you face is totally entrenched around and within you.

In fact, you've been under attack your entire life. Demons have been conducting stealth missions to undermine you ever since you were born. And as you wake up and actively resist and counterattack, the enemy's effort only intensifies. Because he's scared of you!

Why is that? And how do you fight back?

That's what we'll hit next.

CHAPTER 6

Killer and Victim

Okay. Time for another illustration. Imagine it with me:

Here we are, folks, at a championship wrestling match.

(Now stay with me on this. Don't skip ahead a few pages, or close the book and run out on me, just because you don't care for wrestling as a form of entertainment. Besides, you *can't* quit; you're one of the contestants.)

The dingy, smoke-filled hall is packed. Standing room only. **And it's loud.** The fans are all out tonight, and they're screaming for blood.

Over on the wall, there's a sign. Dozens of rows of little light bulbs on a big black background. The lighted bulbs spell out the announcement of the first fight: Satan vs. You!

FIRST DECISION

You walk down the ramp to the ring. The crowd erupts in noise. It sounds mostly like jeering and booing. They must all have their money on Satan.

You walk to the edge of the ring, climb over the ropes,

and stand in your corner. To loosen up, you roll your shoulders and do some air-jabbing and some prancing footwork.

The referee's in the ring, and he's watching you. You detect a touch of disgust in the look he's giving you.

Now here comes your opponent. Satan struts down the ramp, wearing a flashy red cape. The crowd goes wild with cheers.

He's followed by a horde of demons. They're cheering too.

Satan looks three or four times your size and weight. At least. Plus, his shoes and boxing gloves are spiked. The spikes look razor sharp. So do his teeth. And man **is he ever ugly.** His looks alone could kill.

With a single bound he vaults over the ropes into the ring.

So do all the demons. And you notice they're all armed to the teeth with every weapon known to man.

You're thinking this may not be a fair fight.

But here you are. And you're stuck (because I said you couldn't leave).

You take off your sweats. You nervously swat one gloved fist into the other. Your knees are trembling a little.

Satan removes his red cape. His demons aim their weapons. They're calm as can be.

You step to the center of the ring.

So does he, with his monsters close behind.

A bell dings. And the fight begins.

Suddenly, out of nowhere, someone comes charging

over the ring in a flash of light. It's Jesus! He speaks a word. Or maybe it's only a breath. Suddenly Satan and his demons are writhing in pain on the floor. They shriek and howl. They quickly slither under the ropes and along the ramp. As they leave the hall, Satan looks over his shoulder and snarls at you: "We'll be back."

You're alone in the center of the ring. **Standing tall.**

The referee looks at you with saucer-eyes. Apparently he somehow missed seeing Jesus.

He comes over and raises your arm. You're the winner.

The crowd has grown quiet.

You're about to climb out of the ring. But you look up at the sign in electric lights, announcing the second fight of the evening.

It's the World vs. You!

"Stick around," the referee barks at you. He's got that look of disgust again.

SECOND DECISION

Your opponent comes rushing down the ramp. Or "opponents," I should say. There's a crowd of them. Every disreputable type you can imagine. Pushers, prostitutes, pimps, and porno peddlers. Shady marketers selling shady deals. Gurus and sages plugging false religions. Professors and philosophers teaching empty theories. Experts uttering distorted "facts."

What's the deal?

They come forward fast. The crowd is stoked again, cheering madly.

The contestants pour over the ropes from all sides. They're yelling at you, poking you, jabbing you. **They're pressing in, squeezing you.** They aim to strangle you and trample you.

Then—the light again. Jesus again. A simple word again.

Suddenly all these people go moaning and melting down into the ground like the Wicked Witch of the West, leaving only little wisps of smoke curling up from where they once stood.

Again, you're left alone in the center of the ring.

The referee stares at you once more in amazement. He raises your arm as the hushed crowd looks on.

THIRD DECISION

Before you start to step away, you take another look at the sign in electric lights. It's announcing the evening's third fight.

It's You vs. You!

Now how will this work?

And who's the crowd betting on this time?

But the crowd is hurriedly leaving. They're not interested anymore.

The referee leaves too.

And all the lights go out except one bright bulb dangling over the ring.

Everything gets perfectly still and quiet.

You're by yourself.

This fight is yours alone.

You against you.

And in the vast dark silence of the hall, you call out... *"Jesus?"*

CRITICAL BATTLE INFORMATION

Okay, so don't press the details too far in that story.

But here's my point.

There are a few really vital things to know about this war, this spiritual battle we're in.

1. Jesus already won the battle against Satan

Satan is already defeated.

Jesus defeated him on the cross. By His death, Jesus was able to "destroy the one who has the power of death, that is, the devil."[33]

That's why, as the time came for His death on the cross, Jesus could confidently say, "The prince of this world now stands condemned."[34]

And it's why we read in Scripture, "The reason the Son of God appeared was to destroy the devil's work."[35]

I loved the scene in the movie *The Passion of the Christ* that showed Satan writhing in agony and exploding in light as he's finally conquered and crushed by Jesus. Jesus won that victory on the cross—then confirmed it without a doubt by rising from the dead.

There are people who say Jesus didn't rise from the dead. That His resurrection is just a made-up myth. But you can be sure **Satan knows the risen Christ is a cold hard fact.** And he knows that it means he himself is doomed.

Sure, the devil still roams around trying to devour people. God allows him to do that for His own good reasons (until the end comes, when he and his demons and servants will be thrown into the lake of fire.[36]) But THE most important fact about Satan is that he's a *loser*. And Jesus is the Winner.

Can I give you any better reason than that to stay close to Jesus? In this world where Satan still roams, why stray out on your own? Stay hand-in-hand with Jesus, the One who totally has Satan's number, and there'll never be any reason to fear.

Christ's defeat doesn't mean we can be passive when it comes to Satan. We're still called on to stand up to him: "Resist the devil, and he will flee from you."[37] But **the whole reason we can resist the devil is that Christ has already beaten him.** He flees from us because he sees Christ's power in us, the power of the One who's destroying him.

2. Jesus already won the battle against the world

Jesus said it: "I have overcome the world."[38] Again, those words were spoken just before Jesus went to the cross to die. By His death, Jesus conquered the world's system of evil. The world's evil is a defeated power.

That's another outstanding reason to stay close to Jesus. As you walk through this evil-saturated world, don't drift away from Jesus, the only One who can take you clean and undefiled through all this garbage.

Okay, so that takes care of the devil and the world. Their defeat is a fact for us to believe by faith. And we look forward to the day when we see it by sight. There's much, much more we could explore about this. But let's move on.

What about our battle against the flesh?

3. Jesus gives us the ability to win against our flesh

In this part of the war, the dynamics are a bit different.

When we're fighting our flesh, we still look to the death and resurrection of Christ for the victory. But the path to our total victory depends big-time on the actions we take.

It means crucifying the flesh.[39] It means putting the flesh to death.[40]

So in this battle against the flesh, there's **dying to do.** Because our "flesh" is such an ingrained part of us. We're the victim, so to speak. But we're also the killer. Each of us is a "new creation" in Christ,[41] a new person entirely, and that new person is the one who puts to death the old person within us.

Fortunately, even here we don't have to depend on ourselves. Putting the flesh to death requires our active reliance on the Holy Spirit who lives in us.[42] In this wrestling match, He'll be our coach...and much more.

Are you ready to be a trained killer? Of your own flesh? That's what we're ready to learn about now.

CHAPTER 7

Death to Self

When I'm on a speaking tour, alone in a hotel room at night, I'm tempted to watch inappropriate things on TV. It's not easy to change the channel or fast-forward the video. But when I do, I'm putting my flesh to death.

I love hip-hop music. But I have to limit my listening to certain rappers, because if I'm exposed to too much, I'm tempted to start using their profanity. Music is very important to me, so this can be a hard sacrifice. But when I make it, I'm putting my flesh to death.

Putting our flesh to death means letting go of anything or any value that blocks our pursuit of God. It's being willing to sacrifice anything of this world on the altar in love for Christ.

For a martyr, that means letting go of physical life.

But for most of us, the challenge more often is to put Christ and eternal values first in our daily lives, sometimes at the expense of our earthly pleasures, comforts, possessions, and rights.

This is what Paul was saying when he told us to give

our bodies—that is, our whole lives—as a "living sacrifice" to God.[43]

Some people call this "dying to self." And it can be pretty painful. We feel our "rights" are getting stepped on. We're thinking, *I don't need this.* It cramps our style.

God is nudging us to do something, but we really don't want to. So we line up our excuses: After all, I'm tired. After all, I've got to take care of myself. After all, I need a break.

It's about me, me, me. That's our flesh talking.

But God is saying it's all about Him. And all about others. The *me* in us needs to be put down. Put to death. Crucified.

And that gets hard. Super-hard. And honestly, I have a tough time at it.

WHAT IT ISN'T

So what does this die-to-self business look like?

First let's talk about what it *doesn't* look like.

Dying-to-self doesn't mean passively submitting to another person's dominant control in your life. Going along with his or her constant demands and whinings. Being manipulated. This is usually nothing more than feeding your own selfish "need to be needed."

Dying-to-self doesn't mean wimping out on responsibilities and commitments to other people and using the excuse that God is first, not them. That's just a selfish cop-out. It hap-

pens in many Christian homes when a someone neglects
their marriage or family in the name of work or ministry.

*Dying-to-self doesn't mean mentally beating yourself up
with guilt when your conscience convicts you of sin.* Trying to
punish yourself for disobedience. This kind of self-abuse is
just a selfish attempt to try to pay for our own sins (so we
get the pride and glory). But Jesus already made that pay-
ment. (He gets all the glory!) That's why our
self-punishment is so offensive to God. It's **a slap in
the face** of the crucified Christ. It keeps us from enjoy-
ing the Lord's forgiveness and close friendship.

Dying-to-self doesn't mean rejecting God's blessings. Lots of
Christians think they should deprive themselves of *anything*
that's fun (or most of it, anyway). But God your Father
wants you to enjoy the incredible overflow of good things
He sends your way. That includes true pleasures in this
world. Even more important, it includes the joy and spiritual benefits of walking close to Him. Dying to self doesn't
decrease God's flow of blessings. Rather it opens the flood-
gates wider as we become more receptive to the best He
wants to give us.

That doesn't mean I endorse the so-called "health and
wealth gospel." In fact, I think the flashy televangelists who
promote prosperity theology are hypocrites who prostitute
the gospel. They probably don't know the first thing about
dying to self.

"Blessed are you who are poor," Jesus said.[44] *Blessed*
means "happy." He makes sure that some of the poorest

people in the world are among the happiest. But while wealth has its dangers, there are many wealthy people who know how to die to themselves and to this world even as they steward its riches for God's kingdom.

Dying-to-self doesn't mean living your whole life by following negative rules. "Don't do this." "Don't do that." Don't, don't, don't. That kind of approach turns into deadly legalism fast. And it ultimately has no real effect on controlling our sinful flesh.

The Bible has some surprising instructions about this: "Why do you keep on following rules of the world, such as, 'Don't handle, don't eat, don't touch.' Such rules are mere human teaching about things that are gone as soon as we use them. These rules may seem wise because they require strong devotion, humility, and severe bodily discipline. But they have no effect when it comes to conquering a person's evil thoughts and desires."[45]

I'm not saying we're free to live with no rules and no restrictions. But lots of Christians are content to live by rules **while keeping God out of the picture.** (And while conveniently forgetting any of His rules they don't personally like!)

The fact is, dying to self is *not* ultimately about rules; it's about the right *relationship* with God. A dynamic relationship where He's real enough to us to show us (from the Bible and through His Holy Spirit's presence) what to do or not do in every situation.

The fact is, if you decided to live your whole life just by

rules and principles and guidelines, you could never come up with a long enough list. To live the kind of life God wants you to live, you could never record all the regulations you need. Life is too complicated. Every situation is too unique. God will *use* all His laws and principles in the Bible to guide you and show you the true standards and the real issues. But you need *His fresh and active presence* to show you *how* to apply those things in the challenging new situations that come your way every day.

That's why life is such an adventure! That's why you need the living Lord (and not just a rulebook)! As you live in Him and live in His Word (the Bible), He can be depended on to show you the right action to take every time.

WHAT IT IS

So what does *real* dying to self look like?

It means saying no to whatever your flesh is telling you to do in opposition to what God says. (And our flesh finds all kinds of ways to resist Him.)

It means constantly letting go of what your flesh wants to hold on to when God says surrender it. (And our flesh never willingly surrenders anything.)

Above all, it means keeping your life-focus on Jesus. (And your flesh would rather look *anywhere* than at Jesus.)

Is Jesus actually real to you, at this very moment? Do you sense His presence—right now?

If not, then the first aspect of dying to self is removing

whatever obstacles are keeping you from sensing Christ's presence. Admit you're out of touch with Him. Admit this is your fault, not His. Confess how you've let other things distract you. Confess your heart's coldness and hardness. Confess your mental dullness.

Come clean about how needy you are. Go ahead and die to your selfish pride.

Remove the obstacles and distractions. Go ahead and die to your selfish preoccupation with other things instead of with the One who created you and saved you and loves you.

Own up to it all.

Do that—and keep doing it as often as you need to—and you've for sure learned well the first lesson in dying to self.

And then He'll lead you into **even more dying.**

PICTURE YOURSELF

As your Lord leads you down this path, you'll be consciously saying no to this world's values. And fixing your mind on the values of eternity.[46]

You'll be looking out for the interests of others as much as your own.[47] Letting the other person go first. Speaking up to defend those who are being treated unjustly. Moving beyond your own security and your own comfort zone in order to reach those who need help. Bearing others' burdens. Forgiving others. Being patient with others.

Instead of sharing in evil, you'll be exposing it.[48] Confronting what's wrong, even when doing so puts you at risk.

You'll be abstaining from what's wrong and pursuing holiness instead.[49] Ignoring a crass joke. Changing the channel when trash comes on. Averting your eyes when you're tempted to mentally undress an attractive girl or guy. Not taking that first drink if you know you couldn't stop. Avoiding compromising situations, even at the expense of your finances, reputation, rights, or relationships. And if you're single, staying pure—which is more than not having sex with your girlfriend or boyfriend, however much you'd like to cross that line.

You'll be overcoming evil with good.[50]

A friend of mine works for a restaurant where his fellow workers used to tell off-color stories and put down women. He doesn't blast them by saying, "You're going to hell!" He just lives with integrity, going quietly about his business. The other guys have started calling him Superman. "You're like Clark Kent. You don't do anything wrong." Now they've stopped using God's name in vain around him. Or if they do, they apologize.

This guy dies to the world a little every day. And he's got a life that's contagious!

In dying to self, you'll also be learning how to focus your time and energy more tightly on God's specific will and purpose for your life. You'll learn to say no not only to bad things, but even to good things that can get in the way of God's specific best for you.

The world is full of good things that can become distractions…like money, possessions, relationships, sports, entertainment, comfort, convenience. Any of these things can be abused or gripped too tightly. Dying to self means being willing, if necessary, to give up any and all of them.

Dying to self will also mean courageously **pushing forward in what you know God has called you to do.**

That's something my friends Craig Gross and Mike Foster have to practice all the time. They founded XXXchurch.com as a radically new type of ministry, reaching out to people taken down by pornography. As they've brought their message of purity and integrity into churches, conferences, and even porn conventions, they've sacrificed their reputations in the eyes of some churches. They've taken a lot of heat from those who think outreach means bringing the lost into our safe church fortresses. But Craig and Mike are taking up their crosses daily and following Jesus because Jesus told us to go out and win the lost.[51]

A DIFFERENT WAR

In our fight against evil, we don't fight as the world fights. "For though we live in the world, we do not wage war as the world does."[52] "We are human, but we don't wage war with human plans and methods."[53]

The war we're in is a spiritual conflict. And it's ultimately God's battle, first and last. So we fight with His weapons, using His strategy.

That's why, amazingly enough, "dying" is such a big part of it. Dying to self. Putting to death our flesh.

So go ahead.

Pull the trigger on your selfish desires. Tighten the noose around your self-centered longings. Put your pride in the electric chair and flip the switch.

Do it as often as you need to.

Which—as we're about to discover—happens to be pretty often.

CHAPTER 8

Die Daily

A few years ago, a soldier at an army base in North Carolina made his very first parachute jump. And with **no training.**

It was all a mistake. Jeff Lewis was only a supply clerk. But because of a clerical error, his records indicated he was trained and qualified as a paratrooper.

When it was time for a group of his fellow soldiers at Fort Bragg to go up for a jump, Jeff was included. He simply followed orders, as good soldiers do. He went with the flow. "I wasn't going to question it," he said. "I had a job to do, and I had to believe in what I was doing."

Here's what happened, according to the newspaper account:

Before his jump, Lewis attended a one-day refresher class for airborne-qualified soldiers who have not jumped in at least six months. But the class is not meant as a crash course in how to parachute.

Lewis stepped out of the aircraft with the wrong foot, and his equipment got twisted up. But he remembered what the jumpmasters had said at the refresher class and kicked his feet, getting the canopy open....[54]

Fortunately, this guy landed without injury. But that night he was shaken up enough to tell his platoon sergeant the truth about his background.

A few months later, Jeff Lewis graduated from Fort Bragg's Airborne School—thereby becoming fully qualified at last to make his first "official" jump.

I like this guy. I like his go-for-it attitude.

I also like how, after that "unofficial" jump, he decided to get things squared away. He went on and received the training he needed. Reflecting back on that first experience in parachuting, he probably figured that what little instruction he did receive (in that refresher class) was all that kept him from getting killed.

Training is a good thing.

CAPTURING YOUR SOUL

And good training works.

That's a common observation from people who describe their first jump from an airplane. Especially when they recall the critical moment of leaping out the door, and the seconds just after.

Like the memories from this guy:

"The jumpmaster looks me in the eye and asks if I'm ready to skydive. What am I going to say? We're at exit altitude, we've been trained... 'Yes,' I say, louder than was necessary. The door opens all the way; there's more wind and noise than I'd expected... I get the initial command, 'Stand by!'... My brain kicks into gear. This is what the training was for; this is what I am here for."[55]

And this young woman:

"We were now almost on the spot and Jimmy [the jumpmaster] signaled the pilot to cut the engine, which he immediately did. This slowed the plane down to about seventy five miles an hour. Jimmy tapped me on the foot, which I knew meant, 'Any minute now.' It seemed like only a few seconds later he looked me straight in the eyes and yelled, 'Get out there!!' I didn't even think about it. My reaction was automatic. This is what we'd been told would happen. It was the training kicking in without my conscious knowledge."[56]

And this soldier, who battled fear of heights:

"The red light turns green. 'Go! Go! Gooo!' One jumper goes out the door, then another, and a third. I shuffle closer to the door. I'm close, maybe eight feet away. There go the fourth and fifth jumpers in an unbroken line. I'm next. Then—I freeze. I can't move. Everything shifts to slow motion.

"Suddenly, the three jumpmasters shift their focus from the line of jumpers to their one immediate obstacle—me. Their screams barely register as garbled moans. 'Goooo!!! Gooooooo!!!' In a flash, six hands reach out, grab me, and fling me outside the plane.

"I went through the door too quickly to remember it. The outside sky is cloudy gray mixed with the blinding white light. Events are rushing in a hazy blur.

"The first thing to shake my consciousness is my helmet. It is sitting forward, shoving my glasses hard into my nose, and blocking a strip at the top of my vision. As I reach to fix it, I notice my body locked in the rigid position drilled into each jumper during pre-jump training. The training worked even in the chaos of the previous minute."[57]

And finally, this memory from another young soldier:

"A very salty sweat ran down my face and neck, burning my skin where I had just shaved that morning.... Two red lights had come on, one by each rear door. The countdown had started with the command, 'Stand up.' Something strange had happened. My mind had questioned what was about to take place, and my body had responded without question. To my amazement, I had quickly unbuckled my seat belt and stood up waiting for the next command, 'Hook up.' …Every order was obeyed, and I had become the warrior. No matter what my brain was trying to convey to my body, I no longer had control. The training had captured my soul."[58]

Yes, **effective training can capture your soul.** It lets you do what you're otherwise afraid to do. The right training can prepare you to die—to take the leap into dark nothingness—and to do it the way you're supposed to do it. So that after that leap, you can experience life as never before.

WORKOUTS FOR DAILY DYING

So what kind of training do we need for learning how to die to self?

First, here's an all-important truth to drill into your soul:

Jesus says we need to die *every day*. "If anyone would come after me, let him deny himself and take up his cross *daily* and follow me."[59]

Have you done any dying today?

The right kind of spiritual training is a big part of the daily dying we're called to do. I want to give you two training exercises to do every day (if you aren't already doing them). Two things to achieve daily, even when—*especially* when—your flesh doesn't feel like it.

Here they are: Read your Bible and pray. (Not necessarily in that order.)

Yeah, I know. You've heard that advice before. Good suggestions, and hard to follow consistently.

But have you thought of them as a way to die?

That's exactly what's happening when your sinful nature is screaming "No way!" but you get into God's Word anyway. When you don't feel like praying, yet you just admit that to God and go ahead and talk with Him anyway—then you're dying to self.

That's death in action. You're being a cold-blooded killer of your flesh. Just like you're supposed to be.

And it's not only death in action; it's *faith* in action. You show that you believe God and listen to God more than you believe and listen to your flesh or the world or the devil.

So pray. Talk with God every day. Anytime you think about it is a good time to pray. But also set aside at least a few minutes each day, away from any other distractions, and devote those just to Him. Tell God anything that's on your heart. Pray for your needs and desires, and for the needs of people you really care about.

There's no formula. It's a conversation. (You don't follow formulas while talking with other people you love, do you?)

Pray before you read the Scriptures. Ask the Holy Spirit to open your spiritual "eyes" to see what God wants you to see. Let Him show you Himself in those pages.

Pray while you're reading, too. Pray the Scriptures back to God. Express these truths in your own language, and as they relate to your own situation.

The Bible is God's playbook for life. You want to know how to live? You want to get to know better this God who calls you to die for Him? Then spend time every day listening to His voice through the Bible. Meet Him there.

The Bible's like your food from God. Don't neglect it by filling your mind instead with junk—mindless TV, vile song lyrics, pornography, or even too much pleasure reading.

Put these two things—prayer and the Bible—at the center of your personal training program. Your daily death program. And don't let go of them.

TWO MORE THINGS

Now here's two more training exercises to work on regularly, all the time. Two more ways to die again and again.

First, move outside your self-centeredness, and find a group of friends who believe the same solid truths you do about God and the Bible. Find a Bible-teaching church. (If you visit a church and the minister teaches from magazine articles and the news headlines, but doesn't crack a Bible, you're in the wrong place.)

Christian friends and a good church give you the

support, accountability, and encouragement you need as you live the adventure. I've figured out how much I need my cheering squad, my home base, where I'm safe and someone knows my heart. You need that too.

Second, start reaching out, making a difference. God will be calling you out of your comfort zones. He wants you to make yourself available to Him, so He can do through you what you could never do on your own.

He may be moving you in these directions a little at a time. They seem like baby steps. That's okay.

That's what happened to me. When I first started speaking publicly for Christ, I was terrified. I spoke only occasionally, to small audiences. Over a few years, my comfort zone has expanded as God has proven faithful and I've grown stronger. Now I'm willing to stand on the front battle lines, with a strongly confrontational message.

God may not call you to public speaking. But He *has* placed you here to make a difference in people's lives. You can't do that if you're not reaching out to them.

FOR THE DURATION

One of my friends started a skate clothing company called Duration. It's especially for old folks like me (I was born way back in 1970) who are still skateboarding after all these years. The people who are in it for the duration.

Are you in with God for the duration?

It starts by training day in and day out. Dying day in

and day out. Spiritual discipline day in and day out.

It doesn't mean you have to be perfectly good at it all at once. Any skill has to be learned. It takes time, practice, and mental and physical development. The skill of dying to self is no exception.

I'm really into cycling. But I didn't train enough before my first major event—a 250-mile ride over a weekend. By the time I finished, I'd wrecked my knee and injured my Achilles tendon. It took me a long time to rehabilitate. Once I could ride again, I started with short outings—ten miles, then twenty, then thirty, until I could ride one hundred miles a day. That's when I really started having fun.

It was worth it. But it took a lot of patience and work.

When I started surfing, I started with small waves. I had to gain strength and confidence before I started trying the overhead stuff. Even now I don't surf on some beaches because the waves are too dangerous for me. I know my limitations. I'm always pushing myself, but not too fast.

Your skill level in spiritual discipline will increase with time. Be patient with yourself and with God's timing for your growth. Don't set yourself up for failure; set yourself up for success.

But at the same time, never miss a workout!

Our sin nature has a strong survival instinct. It doesn't want to die. The way we learn to effectively kill it is through days and weeks and years of small-but-consistent decisions and practices that build spiritual endurance and strength. **That's the road God wants to take you down.**

By learning and practicing these death-steps every day, you'll be training to take on the bigger challenges later on. When God calls you to really lay it on the line. When spiritual warfare is raging. When the stakes are high. When people are watching. And when God's reputation is at stake.

When that "big" moment arrives, you want to be ready to die for Him. And that readiness comes through dying for Him every day in the "little" ways of regular spiritual discipline.

When the time of crisis comes, your training will kick in. As you take the plunge into an unknown situation where God has led you, you'll let your training guide you. You'll know how to listen for *His* voice instead of your own. Even when there's chaos, you'll stay true to Him. You'll do it even when you're being attacked or tempted by the enemy as never before.

You'll be able to say, as those parachutists did, "This is what my training was for; this is why I'm here." You'll know your training has worked.

And you'll know your training has captured your soul.

CHAPTER 9

Your Funeral Was Yesterday

Imagine you're paging through a newspaper one morning. You're hunting for the sports section. It isn't where it usually is. One of life's little irritations.

While you search, you happen to hit the obituary page. And you stop cold.

Right there's a story about *your* death. There's even a picture. Yep, that's your photo all right. But what's this all about? (You don't usually read the obituaries; maybe you should more often.)

The little article includes details about your funeral. (Except it doesn't say how many people attended; you're hoping lots.)

You stare and stare at it. This comes as **a bit of a shock.**

You fold the paper and set it aside. (You've forgotten all about the sports section.)

You're still breathing—you consciously take note of that fact. You press your wrist to feel your pulse. You run to the

mirror and check your reflection. You look great, actually.
Or at least normal. Definitely not dead.

There must be some mistake.

Well—maybe, maybe not.

MYSTERY ANGLE

I gotta tell you, this whole business of dying to self and of
dying as the doorway to living—it has its mysterious side
for sure.

One of the most mysterious angles is this:

You died.

Already.

That's what the Bible tells us.

God says it: "You *died*...."[60]

The New Testament keeps insisting that when we
became believers in Jesus, it was the stroke of death for us.
For the "old" us, that is. So that the "new" us could
become alive.

This death of ours means super-freedom of all kinds.

It means freedom from the evil world system: "You
have *died* with Christ, and he has set you free from the evil
powers of this world."[61]

It also changes completely our connection to sin. We
used to be sin's slaves. We couldn't help but sin. But
now...total drastic change:

"Our old sinful selves were crucified with Christ so that
sin might lose its power in our lives. We are no longer slaves

to sin. For when we *died* with Christ we were set free from the power of sin."[62]

It gives us this huge wild hope for beating temptation and sin in our lives. Granted, **it's our only hope--** but it's all we need.

IT HAPPENED

All this death of ours is locked into the death of Christ Himself: "For *you* died when *Christ* died."[63] Something Paul said is what we can now say too: "I have been crucified *with Christ*."[64]

When you watched *The Passion of the Christ,* could you start to feel that you were up there on the cross with Jesus? Dying with Him? Being crucified with Him?

Incredible to think about, isn't it?

Nailed with Him to the cross. Side by side with Him in the tomb.

It's true: **Our death is just as real as His death was.**

It's a done deal. Historic reality. Historic fact.

We can even think of our flesh—our sinful nature—as being lifeless now. "Those who belong to Christ Jesus have nailed the passions and desires of their sinful nature to his cross and crucified them there."[65]

And on the basis of this historic fact from yesterday, your today is super-charged with aliveness. Why? One reason only: Because it's super-charged with the living Christ.

Again, Paul's words are ours too: "I no longer live, but *Christ lives in me.*"[66]

Christ in me. It means the ultimate in life-connectedness with Jesus: "For you died when Christ died, and *your real life is hidden with Christ* in God."[67]

Death with Jesus yesterday. Life with Jesus today.

Like I say, I don't begin to fully grasp how all this works. But it's true. And we can spend a lifetime learning to live out the reality of it.

THE BIG REALITIES

I know I'm giving you lots of heavy stuff in this chapter. I know this gets intense. So please stay with me. It's God's truth about *your* life and *your* death. It's stuff that's often hard for us to grasp, but when it clicks, when it starts coming together for us…we get revolutionized.

Deep stuff, yes, but I know you can handle it. You're not a child anymore. Your heart and mind are big and open wide, and you've got the world's best teacher to fill them—God's Holy Spirit.

So reflect with me a moment on the incredible uniqueness of Jesus' death: "For the death that He died, He died to sin *once for all.*"[68] Here's this *one* death, this one amazing sacrifice—the perfect God-Son dying for foolish, bone-headed sinners like us. It was as one-of-a-kind as one-of-a-kind can get. Unique to the ultimate. Never anything like it before. Never anything like it again.

Yet somehow, in the way you and I believe in Jesus and give ourselves to Him, *we have a part* in that one-time unique death. **We share it. We wear it. We take it on.**

In His death…we die.

So that in His life…we can be raised up. Resurrected. Lifted up alive.

It's just gotta be about the most amazing thing anybody ever heard of. We were in-the-grave dead…so we can be up-from-the-grave alive.

"Now if we have died with Christ, we believe that we will also live with him."[69]

It's THE biggest fact about your past: You died with Christ.

And it makes possible THE biggest reality about your present: Christ is your life.

Plus THE biggest fact about your future: You'll live with Christ forever.

That's it in a nutshell. Yesterday, today, and tomorrow—you died, you're alive in Christ, you'll live forever with Him.

IT WORKED FOR JESUS, IT WORKS FOR US

The way all this life-and-death worked for Jesus is the same way it's supposed to work for us.

Think about it:

"For the death that He died, He died to sin once for all; but the life that He lives He lives to God."[70]

Think about the truth that means for you:
I'm dead to sin.
I'm alive to God.

I die to sin.
I live for God.

The wild adventure of life is made possible by the wild terror of death. Death is the pathway to superlife.

We keep coming back to that, don't we? The adrenaline-pumping skydive of life can happen only after that terrifying out-the-door leap of death.

THEY WERE RIGHT

So that newspaper's right. You're dead. The old you, at least.

You might as well accept it.

"Consider yourselves dead to sin and alive to God in Christ Jesus."[71]

And maybe even go and have yourself a funeral. (Be sure to invite all your friends.)

CHAPTER 10

Trust Him with Your Life

In a high school that turned into a hell, a disturbed gunman held his gun to Cassie Bernall's head. He asked if she believed in God. She answered yes. Then he shot and killed her.

That story swept the nation after the Columbine killings. And I'll bet the moment you heard it, a question popped in your mind:

How would I have answered?

When confessing your God brings death—when faith costs everything—do I really believe?

Do I really trust God?

LOVE PROOF

Trust.

That's really what it comes down to, doesn't it?

Here's what we're hearing from our Creator and Savior: "Trust Me. Ahead of you lies the adventure of all adventures. Jump. I'll catch you."

Do we believe it? When we take that jump out of the airplane door—whatever it means in our situation—will we trust that Jesus is our parachute?

You can quickly answer Yes. But **the real proof** will come when God is bringing down His discipline on you.

One of the best Scripture passages about this is Hebrews 12:4–11. God says there that He disciplines you because you're His child. His discipline proves His love. If you were NOT getting that discipline, it would show you didn't really belong to Him.

And though His discipline is never fun at the time, in the end you'll respect and love Him for it. And see great things in your life as a result.

So when tough things hit you—even as a result of your sin—be encouraged! **Look up and you'll see the hand of your Father reaching down.** Those difficulties are simply the proof that your good Father loves you.

UP FOR THE JOB

When God brings something painful in your life for you to endure, He has a purpose. We don't always see it. In fact, we don't ever see it totally. But even before understanding any of it, we can still know and believe that it will bring something good.

God has incredible plans for you. Amazing things for

you to accomplish. But you'll be ready to do them only after He trains you. That training will sometimes be painful. But just think of every trial as a responsibility entrusted to you by God, preparing you for even greater responsibilities in the future.

The fact is, God entrusts great responsibility only to those who proved faithful with small responsibilities. The bigger tasks seem scary, but just think about the honor of being trusted with them. When God gives you something huge and hard to handle, He's saying that you, in dependence on Him, are up to the job!

That's why you can trust Him.

Just remember: Every time something hurtful happens, it's an opportunity to die a little and live a lot.

PERSPECTIVE ON THE INVISIBLE

More than anything else, this kind of trust, this kind of real faith, means learning to see what normally cannot be seen. Faith means being "certain of what we do not see."[72]

Remember in *The Matrix* where Neo trains in the simulated environments? Combat with Morpheus. Encounters with a pseudo-Agent Smith. Leaping between skyscrapers.

What Neo was learning was how to tell the difference between reality and illusion, so illusion wouldn't fool him. He learned to do what seemed supernatural, to bend the laws of physics. In reality he was only manipulating the imagery of the Matrix. He was only shifting the illusion. He had the capacity to do this all along, but he had to learn to see it.

God wants to teach us along those same lines. He wants to build our faith so we **see the unseeable.**

Then we can repeat this Scripture with confidence: "We look not to the things that are seen but to the things that are unseen."[73]

Did you catch that? We "look" at what is "unseen." The invisible becomes visible.

And what are these invisible things? "The things that are unseen are eternal."[74] They're the things that will *always* belong to Christ and to you and me. Not stuff in this world, but things that last forever.

If you tend to get discouraged with tough times, the key to pulling out of it is to focus on what you've been missing. The unseeable, eternal realities of your situation.

The secret is always in our perspective.

PAIN FROM SIN

I mentioned how our training is often painful. But some of the pain God lets into our lives is a direct result of our sin.

If you're in that situation (God's Holy Spirit will make it clear to you), then identify the sin, confess it, receive forgiveness, and take steps in God's power to change it.

That's why it's important to examine your heart regularly

before God. Especially when you're hit by painful times. Check to see whether you brought the pain on yourself by your foolishness.

In my biking, I experience two kinds of pain. If I push myself too hard and injure myself, that's destructive. It's a result of my own foolishness. But if I keep my workouts within reasonable bounds, I'll still be sore, yet it's constructive because it's building strength and endurance.

When I'm speaking in public, I have to be careful. If I say something stupid and unnecessarily offensive and I make people angry, it does no good. I've behaved out of pride. And it hurts me to see their reactions.

When I say something truthful and with the right attitude, I can still offend people. (Jesus sure did.) But then I'm doing the right thing, and it will have a good result. I may become an outcast among my peers, but I have the pleasure of God.

The only way to know the difference is to give my heart to God every day and ask Him to show me what's inside me.

WHAT IF I REALLY BLOW IT?

Sin is serious. Deadly. A Christian who lives in sin is always robbing himself of abundant life to a significant degree.

Sin ruins a Christian's testimony and ministry. And it smears the reputation of Christ before the world. That's why I keep the written reference "Psalm 69:6" with me at all times. Here's what that verse says: "May those who hope in you not be disgraced because of me, O Lord, the LORD Almighty; may those who seek you not be put to shame because of me, O God of Israel."[75] It reminds me how my sin can weaken the army of God.

In fact, as I write, I'm grieved by something I've done that inadvertently hurt a friend of mine. I didn't mean to cause pain. But I was careless. I'm doing all I can to correct the problem, but several other friends have confronted me for speaking publicly against sin and yet having this sin in my own life. And they have every right to their anger.

I understand the pain and seriousness of sin. **I struggle daily with temptation,** and my win-loss record is far from perfect.

But know that one of Satan's favorite strategies is to get us down on ourselves. In fact, the word *devil* means "slanderer" or "accuser."

God offers complete and free forgiveness for every sin. His forgiveness doesn't wait until you've paid some penance or until you've been sad for a long enough period of time. His forgiveness is available as soon as you realize you need it and ask for it.

So don't lose hope. Don't let Satan fool you into thinking God wants to shoot you down. God wants you to stand up again, to be strong and courageous, and to keep going.

DEFEAT IS NOT LIVING

One of the saddest things I see is a Christian who lives in defeat. God doesn't want us to stay in defeat. He wants us to become strong and victorious. He's not a God of perpetual guilt. Once you're forgiven, that's final. He leaves your sin behind, and so should you.

No matter what you've done…no matter how badly you've blown it…you can always come back to God. He *wants* you back. He wants you to win. And with God, you can.

I like how dc Talk sings it:[76]

WHAT IF I STUMBLE, WHAT IF I FALL?
WHAT IF I LOSE MY STEP AND I MAKE FOOLS OF US ALL?
WILL THE LOVE CONTINUE?
WHEN MY WALK BECOMES A CRAWL
WHAT IF I STUMBLE, AND WHAT IF I FALL?

...

I HEAR YOU WHISPERING MY NAME (YOU SAY)
MY LOVE FOR YOU WILL NEVER CHANGE (NEVER CHANGE).
WHAT IF I STUMBLE?
WHAT IF I STUMBLE?
WHAT IF I FALL?
YOU NEVER TURN IN THE HEAT OF IT ALL.
WHAT IF I STUMBLE, WHAT IF I FALL?
YOU ARE MY COMFORT AND MY GOD.

QUICK DETOUR

Before going on, let me take a brief detour. I'm writing this book mainly for Christians who know they have eternal life. They've received that gift from Jesus, a gift that He paid for.

But maybe you've never accepted that gift from Him.

This is a good time to pause and consider God's invitation to you. Will you let Jesus take the death sentence for you? Will you let Him pay your way into eternal life, which you can enjoy both here on earth *and* forever in heaven?

No need to pray anything fancy. **Just tell God** in your own words that you want His free gift of forgiveness and eternal life, paid for completely by Jesus.

Then simply take Him at His word. Believe that He keeps His promise. Believe that He has already forgiven you. Believe that He accepts you completely. And show your faith and confidence by thanking Him.

You can claim your new life anytime—right now, if you're ready, or at any time later. God's always listening. The lines are always open.

You can trust Him for that…and so much more.

CHAPTER 11

Die Laughing

Remember that long scroll in heaven we dreamed about? All those millions of names. All those millions of martyrs.

Where are all these people now?

Closer than you think.

They're all around us. Looking down on you and me. You can't see them, but they see you.

At least that's what Hebrews 12:1 seems to tell us.

The verses just before that (near the end of Hebrews 11) tells us about God's people being tortured. Sliced open with whips. Stoned to death. Sawed in half. Stabbed by the sword.

They were martyrs for their faith.

Hebrews 12 continues their story by reminding us that we're "surrounded" by this "great cloud of witnesses."

They're everywhere.

And they're watching *you*. Watching *me*.

What are they seeing? Are they seeing us continue the story that they began so heroically?

INVITED TO DIE

One of the guys whose name is on that long list is Dietrich Bonhoeffer. He was a young pastor and teacher in Germany when Hitler rose to power. He bravely stayed faithful to Christ and to the gospel when the Nazis were crushing the church in Germany with intimidation and persecution.

One of the things Bonhoeffer is famous for is this statement: "When Christ calls a man, he bids him come and die." When Bonhoeffer wrote those words, he was thinking especially about our daily dying to self. For him, the words eventually came true in a physical sense as well.

Midway through World War II, Bonhoeffer had the opportunity to get involved in a plot to assassinate Hitler. He wrestled with the decision. Eventually he became convinced this is what God wanted him to do.

After the plot's failure, the Nazis in 1943 arrested and imprisoned Bonhoeffer. Two years later they executed him—just days before his prison camp was liberated by Allied forces and World War II ended.

I believe that our faithful brother Dietrich Bonhoeffer is one of the people in that "great cloud of witnesses" that now surrounds us. That means he's watching us. **What does he see?** This pastor who echoed Christ's call to come and die—does he see you and me dying daily to self?

And does he see us living life to the hilt as a result?

THIS IS ME

I hope what he and all those witnesses are seeing in me is someone going for the long-term fix. Somebody addicted to real life. Eternal life. Abundant life.

I have a cause. I have a purpose. I have a message. And I'm going to keep speaking about it. I want to give as many people as possible the craving to do what God called them to do. I want to use my earthly days to convince as many people as possible to grab hold of God's gift of life, for which Jesus died. When I finally stand in heaven, I want to see a huge mob of people there because of His work through me.

And if I'm to die while pursuing my calling, I consider it a worthwhile risk. A risk that makes this adventure so exciting.

Is it dangerous to follow Christ and die to self?

Yeah. Sometimes it's absolutely terrifying. But it's so worth it when the power of God comes through…when you're plunging forward, and He uses your risky faith to do something awesome.

This I know from my own experience: Every day on earth I can feel His hand upon me through the influence of His Spirit in me. I'm compelled by His calling, and so I feel that urgency, that purified panic, that all-consuming desire, that junkie-like craving for the fix of doing His will.

I jump out of the airplane every day and throw myself into His hands. Sometimes I get hurt. Sometimes I become depleted and even depressed. Sometimes I'm leaping across the mountaintops. If it's for the sake of Christ, it's all part of the amazing adventure of life.

And so is the future that's waiting for us in heaven. I can't wait to spend eternity with the One who gave His life for me.

That doesn't mean I'm planning to throw my life away. I don't go rock climbing without a rope. I buckle my seat belt when I drive. I wear my helmet when I'm on my motorcycle. I'm not being stupid.

But I'm humbled and honored to be called by God. And I'm sold out to following Christ, whatever that may mean.

Seriously, **what would I lose if I died?** Compared to what I gain?

For some people, the cost seems too high. They turn away from real life. They refuse to "die." I've seen it happen among my friends, and it's sad. I know God's respects our decisions. But so many people just don't understand what they're choosing.

Don't be one of them.

FOR THE LIVING

There's something you may have figured out several pages back. Probably several chapters back: *This book is more about living than dying.*

Living intensely. Living purposefully.

It's the life that means knowing you're on the winning side, because you know the end of the story. It's loyalty to the Commander-in-Chief and to your fellow soldiers. It's winning as many as possible of the enemy's soldiers over to the kingdom of light.

It's living as a rebel—a rebel against your flesh, against the devil, and against the world's sinful system. It's being unpredictable—blessing those who curse you, praying for your enemies, turning the other cheek.

It's pushing forward every day, training your spirit and your body to die, leaving the things of earthly life behind and moving with confidence and joy into abundant life.

It's not easy. But the difficulty is what gives you such a great sense of satisfaction when God brings you through a huge challenge—one that would have been impossible without Him.

That's God's purpose for you. *Life.* Eternal life. But not something you have to wait for. Not even for a moment. It's present tense. Here and now. Having your true and deepest desires gratified *right now.*

It's the adventure of all adventures. The fulfillment of the first of all your dreams. It's the accomplishment of greatness. The highest of highs, because it never ends. It's the 120-mile-per-hour adrenaline plunge, complete with summersaults and spins. It's dangerous and scary.

It's what you're all about. And can't exist without.

Life is the healthiest of all addictions.

It makes you always hungry for the next fix, but never leaves you empty.

This is all you've ever been seeking. This is what you've been wanting since you were born.

This is the message of the Bible, God's purpose for your existence.

LIFE. Getting it is worth whatever it takes.

And all it takes is to *die.*

So go for it. Die shouting. Die rejoicing. Die dancing and singing and laughing.

Show that cloud of witnesses up there that you know what they're all about.

And that when your time comes, you'll be more than glad to join them.

Extra Stuff

DISCUSSION/REFLECTION GUIDE (WITH HELP FOR GROUP LEADERS)

This section can go a long way in helping you get the most benefit out of this book. It's set up to use as a guide to your own personal reflection and application. Or—even better—use it for group discussion with your friends.

There's a lot here to think about. Plus suggestions for how to help make sure your life gets changed, just like you want it to. Let this section help you intensify the way you live for Jesus. Let it help you deepen your willingness to die for Him.

It's easy to follow. Just take it chapter by chapter.

(And if you're a group discussion leader, look at the end of this section for some special help just for you.)

FOR THE INTRO ("GO PHENOMENAL") AND CHAPTER 1 ("WHY DIE?")

The Echo

Think again about these things Ryan said (they're well worth a second look):

You used to think you knew what made you happy. Now you wonder what you're looking for. Life can seem like a job with no job description.

Ever feel like that?

There's more to move on to. So that's exactly what people do.... Always running to the next thing. Always escaping to the bigger thrill. Always needing a still bigger one.

Have you seen that in people around you? Ever seen it in yourself?

There is such a reality as an adventure-filled, crazy, awesome, exciting, scary, terrifying, fun-filled life. A life that delivers all it promises. Purpose and meaning that never let you down.

How much do you believe this? Does it really describe what you want from life? If not—what *do* you want?

The Talk

1. "I've never felt so alive"—in what moments in your life have you ever thought that (or even said it to someone)? What makes you feel far more alive than normal?

2. What (if anything) would you be willing to lose your life for? (Maybe there's nothing at this point; that's fine. Just be honest.)

3. To truly be ready to die for Jesus, what kind of preparation do you think you need?

4. Take a closer look at John 12:23–27. (These are words Jesus spoke when His death was less than twenty-four hours away.) What do they tell you about Jesus' attitude? What do they tell you about life and death?

5. Why exactly do you think Jesus wants us to be willing to die for Him?

And Now the Action

• What is it exactly you want to get out of this book? What are your expectations? It might be good to write this down.

   And even better: Express it as a prayer to God.

   Whatever you're hoping to gain from going through this book—ask God to supply it to you. (And expect Him to! Thank Him ahead of time.)

FOR CHAPTER 2 ("CRAVE THE FEAR")

The Echo

Some high points to read and think about again:

> If it isn't high-end dangerous, if it isn't risky, if it
> isn't scary, it's not really living.... You and I were
> born for excitement and adventure.... Ultimately
> we can be satisfied with nothing less than the
> adrenaline-filled life. Anything less leaves us
> bored.... We need to break beyond protective lim-
> its. To plunge over the edge. To push for the
> impossible. *To crave the fear.*

**Do you believe all this is really true in your case? And
in everyone's case? Or only for high-action personalities
like Ryan?**

> Satan deludes plenty of people into living and
> dying for wrong causes.

Can you think of anyone who fits that description?

> Christ gives you the true longing to give your life
> only for *Him.*... He planted deep inside us the
> desire to spend our entire existence *for the right cause
> only.*... When you became a Christian, God placed
> inside you the desire to live all-out for the Lord.

Do you recognize this desire inside you? Are you convinced it's there? If so...do you know *why* it's there?

"Christ lives in me"—the Bible teaches us to know that fact by faith. He's inside you...Christ as He fully exists.

Do you really *know* this fact, by faith?

The Bible teaches us to know and to say, "We have the mind of Christ." His mind, of course, holds His vision and His strategies for all you can be and do in life.... And by staying connected with Him, we learn to see it all. We think what He thinks.

How have you been learning to think with Christ's mind? How does a person do that?

You can dull that desire [to live all-out for God]. You can choose to hide it, bury it, deny it.

How do Christians sometimes do exactly that?

Why not nurture that desire instead? Why not unleash it? Why not let it explode? Why not let it take you to excitement beyond your wildest dreams?

How exactly can we unleash this desire?

The Talk

1. When are you most bored with life?

2. What kind of limits and restrictions do you especially sense the need to push beyond? Is it right to feel this way about them?

3. How much do you truly appreciate risk, danger, and the actual potential to die?

4. What are you starting to learn about the goals and plans Jesus has for your life? Is much of it still a mystery? What parts of it are coming clear?

5. Take a closer look at John 10:9–11. What is Jesus wanting most to communicate to us here (about Himself *and* about us)?

And Now the Action

- If you're convinced that the Lord your God has placed deep inside you the desire to live your life and give your life *totally for Him*...then make sure you offer Him thanks for this incredibly valuable gift.

- Ryan says, "I know my purpose." And he says, "I was born to testify to the truth…. This statement is my creed, my calling." What is *your* purpose and creed and calling in life? How well do you grasp it? Whatever it is, write it down to the best of your understanding. Keep it with you. Keep thinking about it. And revise it whenever God leads you to.

FOR CHAPTER 3 ("THE LONG, LONG LINE")

The Echo

Reflect on these points again:

> Persecution against Christians is far from over. In fact, it's getting worse…. The number of Christians dying for Jesus' sake is now more than at any time in history

How aware have you been of that fact? Why is it important to know this information?

> If you're hardly aware of this, maybe it's because you're stuck in your culture's deliberate isolation from many aspects of reality.

Is this true to any degree in your own life? In what ways does our culture isolate us from some aspects of reality?

God's plan for this world calls for a certain number of Christians to be put to death for the sake of Jesus. That number is *not* small. It's huge. Enormous. God knows exactly who's on that list, and how many names there are. Until that number's reached—until all the names are checked off—the killing will continue.

How willing are you to have your name on this list?

If you and I honestly admit the basic truth about our lives, and somebody else is stupid enough to kill us for it...does that make us a hero?

What's your answer to Ryan's question?

True believers in Christ love life more than anyone else possibly can. That's because they see and enjoy real life. They recognize God's hand in everything around them. They know God created all life and everything in this world, and that He created it all good. They love it here, while at the same time they're eager to see Jesus in heaven—on His timing, not theirs.

Are you someone who loves life in this way? What are the biggest reasons behind your love for life?

You're thinking, I just don't know if I've got the nerve or the backbone or whatever it takes to really lose my life for His sake—if and when it really comes to that.

Have you ever thought that?

The Talk

1. Do you expect that *you* may be one of the millions of Christians who die for their faith? Why or why not?

2. Why is it wrong for us to *try* to get ourselves killed for Christ?

3. What qualified Stephen to be the first martyr for Jesus Christ? In Acts 6, take a close look at verses 5, 8, and 15. What do they tell us about Stephen? Then look at the summary of his death in Acts 7:54-60. What would you say is most important about the way Stephen died?

And Now the Action

- Take a good long look at www.persecution.org and get better informed about how Christians around the world are being persecuted.

- Express honestly to the Lord the truth about your willingness to physically die for His sake.

FOR CHAPTER 4 ("RISK EXPLOSION")

The Echo

Hear these things from Ryan again:

> Jesus of course is the strong dude with the smile and the scars. He's the one checking us out for the job of being His follower.... And as our boss, He also demands—graciously and lovingly, but firmly—that we be willing to die for Him.

It's true, isn't it?

It's "for My name's sake," Jesus said, that we face persecution and death.

What exactly does Jesus mean by that— "for My name's sake"?

It's just part of what we share when we identify with Jesus. Because the world happens to hate Him and what He stands for. We can all be grateful that He's clear and up front in telling us about it. He tells us that this is reality, and He tells us why.

Why does the world hate Jesus and what He stands for?

Jesus is not just looking for compliant martyr candidates. He's looking for hearts that are passionately in love with Him. He's looking for the kind of obedience-to-the-death that's driven by our consuming worship and devotion to Him. A worship and devotion that are nurtured by seeing Him and hearing Him, and being amazed and awestruck by what we see and hear.

When was the last time you were truly amazed by Jesus?

Get still before Him. Get quiet. Get rid of the distractions. (You know what they are.)

In your relationship with Jesus, what are the biggest distractions?

If you get quiet enough and close enough...the dying part will seem like a privilege, not a burden. Like a joy instead of drag.

What do you think? How "close" to Jesus is close enough so that dying for Him will seem like a privilege?

The Talk

1. Who would you be willing to die for?

2. Will God ever force us to die for Him, even if we aren't willing to?

3. What's something that is "better than life," according to Psalm 63:3? And how do we experience more of it?

4. Look also at Psalm 116:15. How does the Lord view the death of one of His followers?

And Now the Action

- Ryan says, "Do whatever it takes to let Him draw near to you. Do whatever it takes to really get to know Him. Do anything to hear His loving voice." For you—what's the "whatever it takes"?

- The key to being willing to die for Jesus is to actually come to know Him better—to "fall in love with

Him." What will you do *now* in your life to deepen your love relationship with Jesus?

- Ryan offers these good suggestions. Which ones should you be doing now?

— Go away somewhere and don't come back until you've read through the entire New Testament or even the whole Bible—if that's what it takes.

— Or read just one page, or one paragraph, or one line in the "red letters" of the Gospels. Read it over and over and over. Until you know you're hearing His voice.

— Pray for Him to speak to you. Plead for it. Thank Him for it, even before it comes, to prove your faith.

— And remember how He wants to hear your voice, too. So confess your sins.

FOR CHAPTER 5 ("HOSTILE FIRE")

The Echo

Think about these statements again:

Life is not a sport. Life is real warfare. Actual combat. With actual casualties. It's a murderous war because our enemy is deadly.

How accurate is that as a description of life as you've observed it?

If you think this enemy isn't hunting *you*…if you think you haven't really caught his attention…then maybe he's already won a greater influence and victory over you than you realize. That's one of his most common and successful strategies—to make you think he isn't *personally* threatening *you*.

In a normal day, how conscious are you of our enemy's threats?

Millions of Christians spend most of their lifetime unaware that they're even in a war zone. In effect, the enemy has already devoured them.

Does life normally seem like a war zone to you? Is it really supposed to, in your opinion?

I don't know how much credit to give demonic forces…. But I do know that even when demons don't cause the problem, they still try to use it to plant seeds of discontent and bitterness in my heart. If they can catch me hungry or tired or sick or hurt or depressed, they whisper words of doubt into my mind.

How does this compare to your experience?

The evil has also taken over and saturated this world we live in. "The whole world lies in the power of the evil one."

Does this match your own perspective on the world?

The evil also saturates *us*—in our sinful nature. It's what the New Testament calls *the flesh*. It's the enemy within—the part in each of us that keeps wanting to sin.

Does that match your perspective on your natural inner makeup?

This world wants us to soothe and pamper ourselves. This world demands that we stay committed to our selfishness.

In what ways do you detect this kind of influence from the world?

In fact, you've been under attack your entire life. Demons have been conducting stealth missions to undermine you ever since you were born.

Have you ever sensed that to be true? In what ways?

The Talk

1. How would you describe the kind of warfare mentality we should have in life?

2. Ryan reminds us that Satan's goal "is to strip your very life from you. He comes after us only 'to steal and kill and destroy.' He wants to rob us of all the life which the Lord gives us. That's his favorite way to get back at God, his Maker and Judge." What aspects of true *life* do you see our enemy trying to steal or destroy in people around you? Or in your own experience?

3. Rank these in the order of how strongly they tempt you:

   ___ holding on to selfish "rights"
   ___ pride
   ___ lust
   ___ love of comfort and pleasure
   ___ go-with-the-flow complacency
   ___ ? (something else that comes to mind)

4. Take a closer look at 1 John 2:15–17. What does this key passage point out about the evil we face? And what are we told to do about it?

And Now the Action

- If you haven't had the right kind of warfare mindset in the past…what do you need to do to get one?

FOR CHAPTER 6
("KILLER AND VICTIM")

The Echo

Catch these statements from Ryan once more:

> They're pressing in, squeezing you. They aim to
> strangle you and trample you.

**Does the "world" ever seem to be coming at you like
this? When do you feel this way?**

> Satan is already defeated.... Jesus won that victory
> on the cross—then confirmed it without a doubt
> by rising from the dead.

**Satan obviously doesn't want us to think he's already
defeated and doomed. What tricks does He use to try
and make us think otherwise?**

> The whole reason we can resist the devil is that
> Christ has already beaten him. He flees from us
> because he sees Christ's power in us, the power of
> the One who's destroying him.

**If we aren't letting Christ's power be strong in us...what
effect will that likely have on Satan's strategy against us?**

> Jesus said it: "I have overcome the world."... As
> you walk through this evil-saturated world, don't

drift away from Jesus, the only One who can take
you clean and undefiled through all this garbage.

**How does Jesus do this—how can He keep us clean
from the garbage all around us?**

When we're fighting our flesh, we still look to the
death and resurrection of Christ for the victory. But
the path to our total victory depends big-time on
the actions we take. It means crucifying the flesh. It
means putting the flesh to death.

**Are you ready to take on responsibility for putting
your flesh to death? What do you think it takes to be
ready for it?**

Fortunately, even here we don't have to depend on
ourselves. Putting the flesh to death requires our
active reliance on the Holy Spirit who lives in us.
In this wrestling match, He'll be our coach...and
much more.

**If the Holy Spirit's your coach in this struggle, what
should you expect Him to do for you? What should you
ask Him to do?**

The Talk

1. What all did Jesus actually accomplish *in your life* when He died on the cross and then rose from the dead?

2. "This fight is yours alone"—when we're talking about our fight against our sinful and selfish nature, in what sense is that statement true? In what sense is it *not* entirely accurate?

3. What else do you most want to know about how Jesus defeated Satan? To find out more, take a closer look especially at Luke 10:18; John 12:31 and 14:30; Hebrews 2:14–15; 1 John 3:8; and Revelation 12:7–12 and 20:1–10.

And Now the Action

- Are you fully ready to be trained in putting your "flesh" to death? Will you make the commitment to submit to God's training for it? If so, express this to Him in prayer.

FOR CHAPTER 7 ("DEATH TO SELF")

The Echo

Hear it again from Ryan:

> I'm tempted to watch inappropriate things on TV.

Can you identify?

> I have to limit my listening to certain rappers, because if I'm exposed to too much, I'm tempted to start using their profanity.

Can you identify with this—or anything like it?

> Putting our flesh to death means letting go of anything or any value that blocks our pursuit of God. It's being willing to sacrifice anything of this world on the altar in love for Christ.

What's blocking your pursuit of God?

> God is nudging us to do something, but we really don't want to. So we line up our excuses: After all, I'm tired. After all, I've got to take care of myself. After all, I need a break.

Can you identify?

Die-to-self doesn't mean passively submitting to
another person's dominant control in your life....
Die-to-self doesn't mean wimping out on responsibilities and commitments to other people....
Die-to-self doesn't mean mentally beating yourself
up with guilt when your conscience convicts you
of sin....
Die-to-self doesn't mean rejecting God's blessings....
Die-to-self doesn't mean living your whole life by
following negative rules....

**These are all *wrong* ways to try dying to self. Which
ones tempt you the most?**

The fact is, dying to self is *not* ultimately about
rules; it's about the right *relationship* with God.

**What's the *right* role for rules in your relationship
with God?**

Real dying to self...means saying no to whatever
your flesh is telling you to do in opposition to what
God says.

How good are you at saying no?

Real dying to self... means constantly letting go of
what your flesh wants to hold on to when God says
surrender it.

How good are you at letting go?

Real dying to self… means keeping your life-focus on Jesus.

How good are you at getting and keeping the right focus for your life?

Is Jesus actually real to you, at this very moment? Do you sense His presence—right now?

What's your answer to that question?

In dying to self, you'll also be learning how to focus your time and energy more tightly on God's specific will and purpose for your life. You'll learn to say No not only to bad things, but even to good things that can get in the way of God's specific best for you.

What "good" things are most likely to get in the way of God's specific best for your life?

Dying to self will also mean courageously pushing forward in what you know God has called you to do.

What's the most important thing God has called you to do?

The Talk

1. As we die to self, Ryan tells us to picture ourselves doing each of the following things. Select at least five on this list. Hold each image in your mind—and describe what it looks like in your life, in your real world. Think of something specific and practical:

    — consciously saying no to this world's values...
    — fixing your mind on the values of eternity...
    — looking for the interests of others as much as your own...
    — letting the other person go first...
    — speaking up to defend those who are being treated unjustly...
    — moving beyond your own security and your own comfort zone to reach those who need help...
    — bearing others' burdens...
    — forgiving others...
    — being patient with others...
    — instead of sharing in evil, exposing it...
    — confronting what's wrong, even when doing so puts you at risk...
    — abstaining from what's wrong and pursuing holiness instead...
    — overcoming evil with good...

2. Here are some of the best passages to explore on putting your flesh to death: Romans 13:11–14; Galatians 2:20 and 5:16–26; and Colossians 3:1–10. Notice especially what they say about your own responsibility.

And Now the Action

- If Jesus isn't real to you at this moment, immediately follow this instruction from Ryan: "Admit you're out of touch with Him. Admit this is your fault, not His. Confess how you've let other things distract you. Confess your heart's coldness and hardness. Confess your mental dullness. Come clean about how needy you are. Go ahead and die to your selfish pride."

- "Remove the obstacles and distractions. Go ahead and die to your selfish preoccupation with other things instead of with the One who created you and saved you and loves you." Has God brought something to mind that He wants you to let go of or get rid of? Do this right now. Make the decision before God. *Do whatever it takes.*

FOR CHAPTER 8 ("DIE DAILY")

The Echo

Worth hearing again:

> Here's an all-important truth to drill into your soul: Jesus says we need to die *every day*.... Have you done any dying today?

What's your answer?

I want to give you two training exercises to do every day...even when—*especially* when—your flesh doesn't feel like it. Here they are: Read your Bible and pray. (Not necessarily in that order.)

Not so complicated, is it?

Have you thought of them as a way to die? That's exactly what's happening when your sinful nature is screaming "No way!" but you get into God's Word anyway. When you don't feel like praying, yet you just admit that to God and go ahead and talk with Him anyway—then you're dying to self. That's death in action. You're being a cold-blooded killer of your flesh. Just like you're supposed to be.

Can you do that? Day after day after day?

And it's not only death in action; it's *faith* in action. You show that you believe God and listen to God more than you believe and listen to your flesh or the world or the devil.

Have you got this much faith?

When the time of crisis comes, your training will kick in. As you take the plunge into an unknown situation where God has led you, you'll let your training guide you. You'll know how to listen for *His* voice instead of your own. Even when there's chaos, you'll stay true to Him. You'll do it even when you're being attacked or tempted by the enemy as never before.

Have you seen this kind of effect from training in any other area of your life?

The Talk

1. A big reason for pushing forward with this spiritual training is to be ready for what God wants to do with you in the future. "By learning and practicing these death-steps every day, you'll be training to take on the bigger challenges later on." What are some good ways to get your mind ready for what God wants to do with you in the future? And your body? And your emotions?

2. If it was illegal in this country to read the Bible
    and to pray in the name of Jesus Christ, and
    those laws were vigorously enforced...how hard
    would that make it for you to go on reading
    Scripture and praying?

3. What assignments in the future would you
    most like God to give you? How can you get
    yourself ready for them (just in case He brings
    them your way)?

4. Look in 2 Corinthians 4:10–11 at how Paul
    talked about dying daily. Then look at the
    larger context of that passage—2 Corinthians
    4:7–12. For Paul, what was the big deal about
    dying to self?

5. Why does Jesus want *you* to be willing to die
    daily for Him?

And Now the Action

•   Ryan's counsel in this chapter is to put prayer and the
    Bible at the total center of your personal training pro-
    gram ("your daily death program"). Follow that
    instruction closely, if you aren't already. Use these
    guidelines especially:

— "So pray. Talk with God every day.... There's no formula. It's a conversation."

— "Pray before you read the Scriptures. Ask the Holy Spirit to open your spiritual 'eyes' to see what God wants you to see. Let Him show you Himself in those pages."

— "Pray while you're reading, too. Pray the Scriptures back to God. Express these truths in your own language, and as they relate to your own situation."

• Also this: "Move outside your self-centeredness, and find a group of friends who believe the same solid truths you do about God and the Bible. Find a Bible-teaching church." Have you done that?

• And this: "Start reaching out, making a difference. God will be calling you out of your comfort zones. He wants you to make yourself available to Him, so He can do through you what you could never do on your own." How exactly are you reaching out to others? How is God leading you to do this? (Be alert. Let Him show you!)

FOR CHAPTER 9
("YOUR FUNERAL WAS YESTERDAY")

The Echo

Think again about these things:

When you watched *The Passion of the Christ,* could you start to feel that you were up there on the cross with Jesus? Dying with Him? Being crucified with Him?

How would you answer that?

When we became believers in Jesus, it was the stroke of death for us. For the "old" us, that is. So that the "new" us could become alive.

In your own words, why exactly is this such good news?

It means freedom from the evil world system: "You have died with Christ, and he has set you free from the evil powers of this world."

Do you really feel this freedom?

It also changes completely our connection to sin. We used to be sin's slaves. We couldn't help but sin. But now...total drastic change: "Our old sinful selves were crucified with Christ so that sin might lose its power in our lives. We are no longer slaves to sin. For when we died with Christ we were set free from the power of sin."

Are you convinced that you're no longer a slave to sin? What does it mean for you to claim this truth by faith?

Somehow, in the way you and I believe in Jesus and give ourselves to Him, we have a part in that one-time unique death. We share it. We wear it. We take it on. In His death…we die. So that in His life…we can be raised up. Resurrected. Lifted up alive. It's just gotta be about the most amazing thing anybody ever heard of.

That's actually a fairly simple truth. Why's it often so hard for us to really grasp it, or explain it to others?

The wild adventure of life is made possible by the wild terror of death. Death is the pathway to super-life. We keep coming back to that, don't we? The adrenaline-pumping sky-dive of life can happen only after that terrifying out-the-door leap of death.

In what deeper ways are you understanding this truth more and more?

The Talk

1. What do you think are God's reasons for telling us to think of our sinful natures as being already dead (even when we still struggle with them)?

2. Take a closer look at Romans 6:1–14. This is a critically important passage to study in our fight against the flesh. Can you see why?

3. What practical difference should it make if we think of ourselves as essentially being "dead to sin" but "alive to God in Christ Jesus," as Romans 6:11 says?

4. Why does Jesus want you to know that *you* died when *He* died?

And Now the Action

• What changes in your thinking need to take place so that you really do think of yourself as being "dead to sin" but "alive to God in Christ Jesus" (Romans 6:11)? Express this in your own words. Write it down, to help you lock it into your thinking.

FOR CHAPTER 10 ("TRUST HIM WITH YOUR LIFE")

The Echo

Think about these things again:

Here's what we're hearing from our Creator and Savior: "Trust Me. Ahead of you lies the adventure of all adventures. Jump. I'll catch you."

Is that a message you've sensed from God, especially in His Scriptures? Have you sensed Him telling you to trust Him?

When we take that jump out of the airplane door—whatever it means in our situation—will we trust that Jesus is our parachute? You can quickly answer Yes. But the real proof will come when God is bringing down His discipline on you.

In what ways have you been experiencing God's discipline?

His discipline proves His love. If you were NOT getting that discipline, it would show you didn't really belong to Him. And though His discipline is never fun at the time, in the end you'll respect and love Him for it. And see great things in your life as a result.

In what ways have you learned to appreciate God's discipline?

God has incredible plans for you. Amazing things for you to accomplish. But you'll be ready to do them only after He trains you. That training will sometimes be painful. But just think of every trial as a responsibility entrusted to you by God, preparing you for even greater responsibilities in the future.

What are now the most important responsibilities God has given you?

When God gives you something huge and hard to handle, He's saying that you, in dependence on Him, are up to the job!

What huge and hard-to-handle challenges has God brought into your life?

Just remember: Every time something hurtful happens, it's an opportunity to die a little and live a lot.

Is this perspective a hard one to hold on to? Or do you find it easy?

Some of the pain God lets into our lives is a direct result of our sin.

What are some of the ways you've seen this happen?

One of the saddest things I see is a Christian who lives in defeat. God doesn't want us to stay in defeat. He wants us to become strong and victorious. He's not a God of perpetual guilt. Once you're forgiven, that's final. He leaves your sin behind, and so should you.

Do you ever tend to hold on to the guilt of your sin? When does this tend to happen?

The Talk

1. When a tough situation comes your way, how hard is it to think of it as discipline from God?

2. What are the most important perspectives for us to have about our sin?

3. Take a close and personal look at Hebrews 12:4–13. What are the most important things to learn from this passage about God's discipline?

4. How has God changed you as a result of His discipline in your life?

5. Why exactly can you truly trust Jesus?

And Now the Action

- Has God brought any discipline in your life that you've had a hard time accepting in the right way? Have you been complaining or resentful? If so, confess that immediately to God. And give Him sincere thanks for His loving discipline.

FOR CHAPTER 11 ("DIE LAUGHING")

The Echo

Going back to these reminders:

All those millions of martyrs.... They're watching
you. Watching *me*. What are they seeing? Are they
seeing us continue the story that they began so
heroically?

**What's the best answer to those questions (as far as
your own life goes)?**

I hope what all those witnesses are seeing in me is
someone going for the long-term fix. Somebody
addicted to real life. Eternal life. Abundant life.

Is that a good description of *your* life in this past week?

I have a cause. I have a purpose. I have a message.
And I'm going to keep speaking about it. I want to
give as many people as possible the craving to do
what God called them to do. I want to use my
earthly days to convince as many people as possible
to grab hold of God's gift of life, for which Jesus
died. When I finally stand in heaven, I want to see
a huge mob of people there because of His work
through me.

How much can you identify with Ryan's words here? How much do you want to be able to identify with him more fully?

Is it dangerous to follow Christ and die to self? Yeah. Sometimes it's absolutely terrifying. But it's so worth it when the power of God comes through…when you're plunging forward, and He uses your risky faith to do something awesome.…

Can you identify with Ryan?

I feel that urgency, that purified panic, that all-consuming desire, that junkie-like craving for the fix of doing His will. I jump out of the airplane every day and throw myself into His hands. Sometimes I get hurt. Sometimes I become depleted and even depressed. Sometimes I'm leaping across the mountaintops. If it's for the sake of Christ, it's all part of the amazing adventure of life.

Can you identify?

Seriously, what would I lose if I died? Compared to what I gain?

Have you thought through that question for yourself? What would you lose if you died? What would you actually gain?

For some people, the cost seems too high. They turn away from real life. They refuse to "die." I've seen it happen among my friends, and it's sad. I know God's respects our decisions. But so many people just don't understand what they're choosing.

Have you seen the same response in people you know?

The Talk

Here's a story to think about:

Picture yourself walking along the street. Someone drives up beside you. He must be rich, because he's in a brand new Corvette. He parks at the curb, gets out of the car, then walks over to you. And he hands you a hundred-dollar bill.

"Here," he says. "I know you didn't earn this. But it's yours. You can spend it however you want."

You're blown away. You tell him thanks.

Then he adds, "Here's my suggestion for how to spend it. Offer it back to me, and I'll give you the Corvette." In his other hand he holds out the title and the keys.

What would you do?

How is that situation a lot like the kind of choice God is offering us with our life?

Think about it: When we give our lives to Him, we really aren't offering that much, are we? Especially when He's the one who gave us every cell and molecule in our existence. (Not to mention saving us from hell.)

What do you think?

And Now the Action

- Remember Ryan's words: "So go for it. Die shouting. Die rejoicing. Die dancing and singing and laughing. Show that cloud of witnesses up there that you know what they're all about. And that when your time comes, you'll be more than glad to join them."

   Can *you* do that?

HELP FOR GROUP LEADERS

You can have a blast guiding a discussion group through this book. While you're helping them get in touch with God's plans for an adventure-filled life, you'll learn tons yourself.

Some quick reminders:

— Encourage everyone to individually read through all of this book. Stay open to whatever questions the group members have as a result of interacting with the content.

— Lots of questions will probably come up. Lots of different opinions might be expressed. Whenever possible, go to the Scriptures together to look for God's answers and perspectives. Use the Scriptures to help keep God in charge of your discussion. Encourage everyone in your group to hear His voice coming through in the pages of the Bible.

— Set an example by responding honestly to the teaching in this book. All of us have a lot of room to grow in learning how to live out this book's message. We'll always need to go farther in these areas. So be candid about your personal need. Face it honestly, and this will encourage the others in the group to do the same.

— Discuss together how you can support and encourage one another in this process of learning how to die to self and how to be willing to physically die for Jesus.

— Pray for these people. Pray together with them, and pray for each of them on your own. Ask God to be at work, and thank Him ahead of time (by faith). Ask His Holy Spirit to be the group's teacher.

— As you pray, ask God to protect this group from disunity, selfishness, and pride. Ask for the Holy Spirit to give all of you spiritual insight into His truths from the Bible. Ask for the personal discoveries and breakthroughs that are needed in each group member's life.

Notes

1. John 10:10 (ESV)
2. John 10:10 (NLT)
3. Matthew 10:39; 16:25; Mark 8:35; Luke 9:24; 17:33; John 12:25
4. Matthew 16:24–25
5. John 12:24 (ESV)
6. John 12:26 (ESV)
7. Revelation 3:15–16
8. John 8:44
9. Matthew 16:25 (NKJV)
10. Galatians 2:20
11. John 14:12
12. 1 Corinthians 2:16
13. Ephesians 3:20
14. John 18:37
15. dc Talk and The Voice of the Martyrs, *Jesus Freaks* (Tulsa, OK: Albury Publishing), 15; also dc Talk and The Voice of the Martyrs, *Jesus Freaks, Volume II* (Minneapolis, MN: Bethany House), 356
16. Paul Marshall with Lela Gilbert, *Their Blood Cries Out* (Dallas, TX: Word), 253–5
17. Matthew 26:53–54 (NLT)
18. Revelation 6:11(NLT)
19. Revelation 7:17 (ESV)
20. Romans 5:7 (NLT)
21. Romans 5:8 (NLT)
22. Matthew 24:9 (NIV)
23. Luke 21:16 (NIV)
24. John 15:20 (NIV)
25. John 16:2 (NIV)
26. Revelation 2:10 (NIV)

27. Matthew 24:9 (NKJV)
28. John 10:10 (ESV)
29. 1 Peter 5:8 (NIV)
30. 1 John 5:19 (ESV)
31. Galatians 5:17–21
32. 1 John 2:16 (NIV)
33. Hebrews 2:14 (ESV)
34. John 16:11 (NIV)
35. 1 John 3:8 (NIV)
36. Revelation 20:10, 14–15
37. James 4:7 (ESV)
38. John 16:33 (ESV)
39. Galatians 5:24
40. Romans 8:13; Colossians 3:5
41. 2 Corinthians 5:17 (NIV)
42. Romans 8:13; Galatians 5:16–18
43. Romans 12:1
44. Luke 6:20 (ESV)
45. Colossians 2:20–23 (NLT)
46. Colossians 3:1–2
47. Philippians 2:4
48. Ephesians 5:11
49. 1 Thessalonians 5:22; Hebrews 12:14; 1 Peter 1:15–16
50. Romans 12:21
51. Matthew 28:19–20; Acts 1:8
52. 2 Corinthians 10:3 (NIV)
53. 2 Corinthians 10:3 (NLT)
54. Associated Press, May 20, 2000. Copyright Athens Newspapers, Inc.
55. Bill Bayley
56. Lola Partain
57. From "The Parachute on My Back: A True Story about Fear";
    Essays and Anecdotes, IdeasandEvents.com Updated February
    15, 2004
58. George Santaguida
59. Luke 9:23 (ESV)
60. Colossians 3:3 (NLT)
61. Colossians 2:20 (NLT)
62. Romans 6:6–7 (NLT)
63. Colossians 3:3 (NLT)

64. Galatians 2:20 (ESV)
65. Galatians 5:24 (NLT)
66. Galatians 2:20 (NIV)
67. Colossians 3:3 (NLT)
68. Romans 6:10 (NKJV)
69. Romans 6:8 (ESV)
70. Romans 6:10 (NKJV)
71. Romans 6:11 (ESV)
72. Hebrews 11:1 (NIV)
73. 2 Corinthians 4:18 (ESV)
74. 2 Corinthians 4:18 (ESV)
75. (NIV)
76. Toby McKeehan & Mark Heimermann, Copyright ©1995 Fun Attic Music/Achtober Songs/Up In The Mix Music (All rights on behalf of Achtober Songs and Up In The Mix Music administered by EMI Christian Music Publishing). As quoted in dc Talk and The Voice of the Martyr, *Jesus Freaks*, 4–5

OUR GENERATION IS BEING DESTROYED BY MANIC TOLERANCE!

1-59052-152-8

Accepting everything means you believe in nothing. When it comes to right and wrong, sitting on the fence won't get you—or the people you love—anywhere. Passiveness is not love. Love is getting in people's faces and telling them the truth.

In his first release, *Be Intolerant,* Ryan Dobson has the courage to point out that some ideas are simply stupid. Honest and unflinching, he will show you how to back up your beliefs and be intolerant—in love.